YORK NOTES

General Editors: Professor A.N. Jeffares (*University of Stirling*) & Professor Suheil Bushrui (*American University of Beirut*)

William Shakespeare

OTHELLO

Notes by John Drakakis

BA MA (CARDIFF) DIPED (EXETER)
Lecturer in English Studies, University of Stirling

LONGMAN
YORK PRESS

The illustrations of the Globe Theatre are from
The Globe Restored in Theatre: A Way of Seeing by
C. Walter Hodges, published by Oxford University Press.
© Oxford University Press

YORK PRESS
Immeuble Esseily, Place Riad Solh, Beirut.

LONGMAN GROUP UK LIMITED
Longman House, Burnt Mill, Harlow,
Essex CM20 2JE, England
Associated companies, branches and representatives
throughout the world

© Librairie du Liban 1980

First published 1980
Thirteenth impression 1993

ISBN 0-582-02291-6

Printed in Hong Kong
WLEE/08

Contents

Part 1

Introduction

The life of William Shakespeare

William Shakespeare was born in Stratford-upon-Avon, a small town in Warwickshire. He was christened in Holy Trinity Church on 26 April 1564, and patriotic enthusiasts, eager to have his birth coincide with the celebration of St George's day (St George is the patron-saint of the English) have suggested that he was born on 23 April 1564. Shakespeare's father, John, had married Mary Arden, the daughter of a local land-owner from the village of Wilmcote to the north-west of Stratford, and by 1564 he had built up a successful business as a glover and merchant. He bought land and houses in Stratford, and in 1568 he was made Mayor. But after 1575 his fortunes declined and he was forced to mortgage some of his property in order to pay his debts.

Little is known of Shakespeare's early life. He probably attended the King's New School in Stratford where he learned to read and write, as well as the rudiments of Latin grammar. In 1582, and at the age of eighteen, he married Anne Hathaway, the daughter of a farmer who lived in the small village of Shottery not far from Stratford. Anne was some seven years older than her husband. On 26 May 1583 Shakespeare's eldest daughter, Susanna was christened, and some eighteen months later on 2 February 1585, his twin children Hamnet and Judith were christened.

The years 1585 to 1592 are usually described by biographers of Shakespeare as 'the lost years' since nothing is known about this period of his life. He may have become a schoolmaster for part of this time, and he may have been arrested for poaching. These are speculations based on hearsay evidence, but it was sometime during these years that he left Stratford for London and for a career in the theatre. Periodically companies of touring players passed through Stratford, and it is possible that Shakespeare joined one of them. We know that, in 1587, one such company, the Queen's Men, were short of an actor, although we have no certain evidence that the person they recruited was indeed Shakespeare.

The first reference to Shakespeare as a professional dramatist is in 1592 when the writer and dramatist Robert Greene referred disparagingly to him as 'an upstart crow' who was 'in his own conceit the only

Shake-scene in a country'. By this time Shakespeare had already written the *Henry VI* plays (from which Greene had quoted in his insulting remarks). In 1593 the narrative poem *Venus and Adonis* was published, and it was dedicated to Henry Wriothesley, the third Earl of Southampton. In 1594 *The Rape of Lucrece*, another narrative poem, was published and dedicated to the same person. It was also probably during the period 1592-4, when the London theatres were closed because of the outbreaks of the plague, that many of the sonnets were written, and some commentators have suggested that Wriothesley is the mysterious 'Mr. W.H.' to whom they were dedicated when they were published in 1609.

By 1594 Shakespeare was a member of the company of actors known as the Lord Chamberlain's Men, which numbered among its ranks actors like the clown William Kempe, and the famous Richard Burbage. We know too that, in addition to writing plays for this company, Shakespeare also acted himself. For example, he acted in Ben Jonson's comedy *Every Man in His Humour* in 1598, a play he was to remember when he came to write *Othello*, and later in Jonson's *Sejanus* (1603) where he may have played the part of Tiberius. Although there is no evidence for it, it has been suggested that he played the role of Adam in his own *As You Like It* (1598-9), and the Ghost in *Hamlet* (1600-1).

The regular playhouse of the Lord Chamberlain's Men was The Theatre, situated in Shoreditch outside the northern boundaries of the City of London, and which had been built by Cuthbert and Richard Burbage in 1576, long before Shakespeare arrived in London. In 1598 this playhouse was dismantled and its timbers taken across to Southwark on the south bank of the River Thames in order to build the Globe Theatre. This is the theatre with which we most associate Shakespeare. He owned a tenth share in the new enterprise, and was thus entitled to receive ten per cent of the profits.

By 1597 Shakespeare had made enough money to buy the house known as New Place, the second biggest house in Stratford. This was the first of a number of purchases of land which he made during the period 1597 to 1605, and records of his various business dealings in Stratford still survive. In 1596, at the age of eleven, his son Hamnet died, while in 1601 his father John also died. In 1607 his eldest daughter Susanna married John Hall, and they may have lived for some time in the cottage now known as Hall's Croft (which currently houses the Stratford Festival Club). After Shakespeare's death in 1616 the Halls moved into New Place.

By 1603, when Queen Elizabeth I died, Shakespeare had written some twenty-four plays and the Chamberlain's Men had become the leading acting company of the time. Indeed, it has been suggested that the play *The Merry Wives Of Windsor* (1600), was written at the request of Elizabeth herself. After the Queen's death the company changed its name to the King's Men, and was in receipt of the patronage of the new king, James I. A year after the King's accession to the throne *Othello* appeared, and was acted before him at the Christmas festivities of that year. It was during the period 1600 to 1607 that Shakespeare wrote the major tragedies, beginning with *Hamlet* in 1600–1, and ending with *Coriolanus* in 1607–8.

In 1608, Shakespeare, along with his business associates the Burbages, John Heminges and Henry Condell (who later jointly edited the First Folio of Shakespeare's plays in 1623), Thomas Evans, and William Sly, leased a small indoor theatre in the City of London called Blackfriars. Some critics have felt that this new building, different in its structure from the Globe, played a large part in the noticeable alteration of Shakespeare's dramatic style at this time. It is argued that plays like *Pericles* (1607–8), *Cymbeline* (1609), *The Winter's Tale* (1610), and *The Tempest* (1611) are the result of Shakespeare's artistic response to a new and more intimate kind of theatre. Unfortunately this argument does not hold, since the first record of a performance of *The Winter's Tale* in 1611 intimates that it took place at the Globe. Also it is known that one of Shakespeare's very last plays, *Henry VIII*, was performed at the Globe because during an actual performance the firing of a cannon set the theatre alight, and burned it to the ground.

After 1613 Shakespeare seems to have written no more plays. His last few years were spent in retirement in Stratford, where he died on 23 April 1616. Popular legend has it that Shakespeare caught a fever after a drinking bout with Ben Jonson and the poet Michael Drayton.

Unfortunately, we do not know the circumstances of his death, but his will survives, and biographers have sought to infer much from its contents. For example, the bequest of his 'second best bed with the furniture' to his widow Anne has prompted speculation about matrimonial disharmony in the Shakespeare household. But his latest, and possibly most reliable, biographer, Professor Samuel Schoenbaum* has suggested that in any event Anne would have been entitled to one-third of Shakespeare's estate, and that the bed may well have had sentimental associations. It seems more than likely that the best bed was reserved for visitors to New Place.

In 1623, some seven years after Shakespeare's death, two of his former partners John Heminges and Henry Condell gathered together his plays in one impressive volume, known as the First Folio. Of the thirty-five plays that this volume contains some sixteen had never before appeared in print.

William Shakespeare: A Compact Documentary Life, Oxford, 1977.

The Elizabethan theatre

Shakespeare was a professional dramatist, and his life therefore revolved very much around the public theatre of his day. In order to understand how his plays work on the stage, we need to have some idea of the kind of theatre for which they were originally written. The Prologue in Shakespeare's history play *Henry V* (1599-1600), tells us what actors and dramatist expected in the way of cooperation from their audiences; spectators are urged to:

> Piece out our imperfections with your thoughts:
> Into a thousand parts divide one man,
> And make imaginary puissance;
> Think when we talk of horses that you see them
> Printing their proud hooves i'the receiving earth;
> For 'tis your thoughts that now must deck our kings,
> Carry them here and there, jumping o'er times,
> Turning the accomplishment of many years
> Into an hour-glass;
>
> (Prologue: lines 23-31)

What kind of theatre could permit so complete an engagement of the imagination? Let us begin by looking at the physical measurements of such a building. The builder's contract for the Fortune Theatre which was erected outside the northern boundary of the City of London in the parish of St Giles' in Cripplegate in 1600, still survives, and is fairly exact in its information. Though the Fortune was a square building, it was modelled in certain crucial respects upon Shakespeare's own theatre, the Globe, and was erected by the same builder, Peter Streete. It contained a rectangular stage which jutted out into 'the yard' of the theatre, and which measured 27½ feet deep by 43 feet wide, similar to that of the Globe. We usually refer to this type of theatre as 'theatre-in-the-round'. In both theatres the 'yard' was open to the sky, providing standing room for part of the audience, while the remainder sat in the more expensive, but covered, galleries set in the outer walls of the building. The stage itself was covered by a large canopy supported by two stout pillars, and usually referred to as 'the heavens'. On the underside of the heavens (that is its ceiling) were probably painted the signs of the zodiac, and the entire cosmological layout of the universe as the Elizabethans understood it. Clearly, Heaven and its position in the universe was not left to the imagination of the audience. Similarly, because the stage stood about four feet off the ground, there was a place for Heaven's opposite, Hell, which was usually reached through a trap-door in the floor of the stage. Thus, the decline of a character like Othello would take place on a stage where both 'Heaven' and 'Hell' were already physically represented, thus adding by implication, a further dimension to the tragic action of the play.

The actors made their entrances and their exits through one of a number of doors situated at the back of the stage. It seems likely that at stage level there were two small doors—one each side of the stage—and a large pair of double-doors in the centre of the back-wall of the stage which, when opened, could be used as an 'inner stage'. It was at the back, and behind these doors, in what is called the 'tiring-house' that the actors changed their costumes, or kept their stage properties. Above the tiring-house was a balcony which was often used in particular

THE GLOBE PLAYHOUSE

The theatre, originally built by James Burbage in 1576, was made of wood (Burbage had been trained as a carpenter). It was situated to the north of the River Thames on Shoreditch in Finsbury Fields. There was trouble with the lease of the land, and so the theatre was dismantled in 1598, and reconstructed 'in another forme' on the south side of the Thames as the Globe. Its sign is thought to have been a figure of the Greek hero Hercules carrying the globe. It was built in six months, its galleries being roofed with thatch. This caught fire in 1613 when some smouldering wadding, from a cannon used in a performance of Shakespeare's *Henry VIII*, lodged in it. The theatre was burnt down, and when it was rebuilt again on the old foundations, the galleries were roofed with tiles.

scenes; for example, Brabantio's entry *'at a window'* in Act I Scene 1 of *Othello* (the Folio text simply reads *'above'*) indicates that he entered through one of the doors leading on to the balcony, to look down at Iago and Roderigo in the street (that is at stage floor level). It is highly ironical that after having satisfied himself of his daughter's absence he re-enters *'in his night-gown, and Servants with torches'* at the same level as Roderigo, thus indicating in symbolic terms the speed of his own decline.

Since there were no artificial lights in the Elizabethan theatre, performances took place during the afternoons. The 'torches' which the servants carry therefore, help to reinforce the impression that the action is taking place at night, although they fulfil an added ironic function in that these torches serve the cause of deception rather than assist in illuminating the truth.

Unfortunately we know far too little about how actors moved and spoke on the stage, although we may safely assume that they did so in ways different from those of modern actors. We should also bear in mind that there were no actresses on the Elizabethan stage; the parts of women were played by highly trained young boys whose voices had not yet broken. Thus the parts of Desdemona, Emilia, and Bianca would have been played by boys, and an Elizabethan audience would have accepted this convention. Also, the stage contained no fixed scenery, and no attempt was made to create the 'illusion' that everyday events were taking place. As the Prologue to *Henry V* suggests, it was the audience which provided, through its own corporate imagination, the 'setting' or background against which the action took place. In any event, the 'localised' settings for particular parts of the action must have been viewed in relation to the universal setting (Man acting out the drama of his own destiny between the opposed forces of 'Heaven' and 'Hell') of which the theatre itself was the supreme symbol. It was not for nothing that Shakespeare's company called their theatre the Globe. This absence of fixed scenery meant that the language of the play became the focus of the audience's attention, since in addition to communicating the states of mind of particular characters, it also provided details of these 'localised' settings. Roderigo's 'Here is her father's house, I'll call aloud.' (I.1.74) is, in this context, a kind of stage-direction, designed to tell the audience where he is, and what he proposes to do. Details of this kind are scattered throughout the play, and they help us to 'place' the action as well as guide our responses to the ways in which particular characters speak and behave. The sheer artificiality of the edifice of the play meant that it was not considered important to imitate closely the language of everyday speech. The intensity and concentration of expression could be varied to suit the requirements of each situation. For example, when Othello speaks poetically, the in-

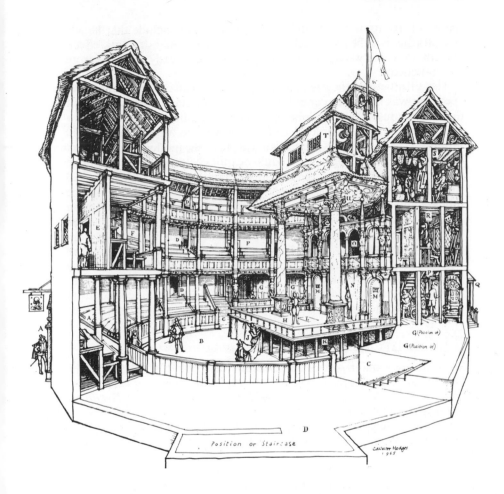

A CONJECTURAL RECONSTRUCTION OF THE INTERIOR OF
THE GLOBE PLAYHOUSE

AA Main entrance
 B The Yard
CC Entrances to lowest gallery
 D Entrance to staircase and upper galleries
 E Corridor serving the different sections of the middle gallery
 F Middle gallery ('Twopenny Rooms')
 G 'Gentlemen's Rooms' or Lords' Rooms'
 H The stage
 J The hanging being put up round the stage
 K The 'Hell' under the stage
 L The stage trap, leading down to the Hell
MM Stage doors

 N Curtained 'place behind the stage'
 O Gallery above the stage, used as required sometimes by musicians, sometimes by spectators, and often as part of the play
 P Back-stage area (the tiring-house)
 Q Tiring-house door
 R Dressing-rooms
 S Wardrobe and storage
 T The hut housing the machine for lowering enthroned gods, etc., to the stage
 U The 'Heavens'
 W Hoisting the playhouse flag

tensity of his utterance should not prompt us to conclude that he is a poet. Rather it is the playwright striving for a particular dramatic effect, something which would receive acceptance and a ready response from the audience.

The Elizabethan theatre was an intimate theatre (for example, no spectator was more than about 60 feet from the stage), despite the fact that a playhouse like the Globe could hold an audience of between two and three thousand people. Because there was no attempt to think in terms of a 'picture-frame', which is a feature of the modern proscenium-arch stage, the large acting area could be quickly transformed from one locality to another. Thus the action was continuous throughout, and the movement from scene to scene resembles, in its speed, that of the modern film capable of moving wherever the requirements of the action dictate. In addition to these physical characteristics, Shakespeare was perhaps more fortunate than some of his fellow dramatists in that from about 1594 onwards, when he joined the company known as the Chamberlain's Men, he was able to write for specific actors whose talents he knew intimately. This relationship was sustained throughout his working life, and represents possibly the most fruitful cooperation of playwright, actors, and theatre in the history of English drama.

The sources of *Othello*

Shakespeare's main source for *Othello* was probably 'The Story of Disdemona of Venice and The Moorish Captain' which appeared in a collection of Italian stories by Giraldi Cinthio entitled *Gli Hecatommithi*, and which was published in Venice in 1566. Here Shakespeare found the bare outline of his plot, but the addition of certain details and the reworking of others give some important clues to his artistic purpose.

In Cinthio's story only Disdemona is named, 'the 'Moorish Captain' (Othello), 'the Ensign' (Iago), and 'the Captain' (Cassio) being referred to throughout by their titles only. Moreover, the action takes place over a much longer period of time than in Shakespeare's play, allowing a sizeable gap between Disdemona's marriage and the Moorish Captain's appointment to the Governorship of Cyprus. From the outset the only objection to the propriety of their marriage comes from Disdemona's relatives who, we are told, 'did all they could to make her accept a different husband'. The Moorish Captain is characterised as 'a man of great personal courage, who, because he had every advantage of person and had given proofs of military ability and lively intelligence, had a high reputation among the nobility', while Disdemona's love for him was due 'not to an impulse of womanly desire, but to a just appreciation of his worth'. Once married, Cinthio observes that 'they lived together in such concord and tranquillity, while they were in Venice, that there was never a word—let alone an act—between them that was not affectionate'.

It is the Ensign who intrudes into this idyllic relationship, 'a man of very fine appearance but of the most depraved nature that ever a man had in the world.' The Ensign falls in love with Disdemona, but believes that she is in love with the Captain (Cassio in Shakespeare's play). He therefore seeks to kill his rival, and vows to turn the Moorish Captain against Disdemona. Cinthio makes the Ensign's love for Disdemona the main motive for his villainous plot, whereas in Shakespeare's play this detail is peripheral. The Captain is deprived of his rank for brawling, and the Ensign (who in Cinthio's story is not jealous of his rival's promotion, and who does not engineer this incident), takes advantage of this to reveal to the Moorish Captain that his wife is adulterous. Meanwhile, the Ensign's three-year-old daughter (who does not appear in Shakespeare's play) steals Disdemona's handkerchief, thus providing the circumstantial evidence which her father will use to convince the Moorish Captain of his wife's guilt. The Captain finds the handkerchief and knowing it to belong to Disdemona, wishes to return it to her. He attempts to, but his visit is used to support the Ensign's allegations against him. Later, the Moorish Captain overhears a conversation between the Ensign and the Captain which is used to intensify his suspicions: 'and putting on an act of astonishment he [the Ensign] contrived by expressive gestures with his head and his hands to seem as though he were listening to extraordinary things.' When Disdemona is confronted with the loss of her handkerchief she is confused and lies, but also, the change in her husband's behaviour causes her, unlike Shakespeare's heroine, to have second thoughts about the marriage:

And I very much fear that I am one who gives an example to young women not to marry against the will of their families. Italian ladies may learn from me not to link themselves to a man whom nature, climate, and manner of life separate from us.

Also, in Shakespeare's play one character, Bianca, is asked to copy the design of the handkerchief, and is the woman whose house Cassio frequents, but in Cinthio's story the Captain's 'woman at home who made marvellous embroidery on fine linen' is different from 'the harlot with whom he used to amuse himself'.

Roderigo does not appear at all in Cinthio's story, where it is the Ensign who agrees to kill the Captain. He also plots with the Moorish Captain to kill Disdemona and to make the murder seem like an accident. He does not succeed in his plot to kill the Captain, but one night the Ensign hides in Disdemona's closet and as she approaches he creeps out and hits her 'a terrible blow in the small of the back' with a stocking filled with sand. After laying her on her bed he splits her head, and he and the Moorish Captain then attempt to conceal the crime by making 'the ceiling timbers of the room fall down, just as they had planned together'. Although the murder goes undetected, the Moorish Captain now begins to realise how much he loved Disdemona and he rejects the Ensign. The Ensign, for his part, seeks to revenge this rejection by informing the Captain that the Moorish Captain had tried to kill him. When the Venetian government hears about these events in Cyprus it recalls the Moorish Captain to Venice and tortures him to find out if they are true, 'But with great fortitude of mind he endured all his torments, and deemed everything with such constancy that nothing could be got out of him'. The Ensign is also tortured, but he ends by dying 'miserably'. The whole of Cinthio's narrative thus becomes a proof of the way in which Providence revenges evil deeds, and he ends by observing that the entire story was revealed 'after his death by the Ensign's wife, who had all along known the truth'.

Shakespeare evidently derived much of the plot, as well as the themes for his play from Cinthio's story. The 'nobility' of the Moorish Captain, and his 'reputation', Disdemona's 'innocence', the sublimity and harmony of their language and its subsequent alteration, are all echoed in the play. The introduction of Roderigo, the gulling of Brabantio, and the final apportioning of the responsibility for Desdemona's murder to Othello himself, indicate a marked shifting away from Cinthio's story as he turned it into a tragic drama.

Cinthio's narrative, however, was by no means Shakespeare's only source. The Chronicles of Hall and Holinshed gave him sufficient material to experiment in the earlier *Richard III* with a prototype of the villainous character of Iago, and with the various methods of engaging the sympathy of the audience for villainy through the judicious use of soliloquy. Also, in *The Rape of Lucrece*, a story popularised in the Middle Ages in Chaucer's *The Legend of Good Women*, and in Shakespeare's own time in Painter's *The Palace of Pleasure* (1566), Shakespeare had begun to explore the kind of colour-symbolism that he later employed in a much more mature way in *Othello*.

In plays such as *Much Ado About Nothing* (1599), and *The Merry Wives of Windsor* (1600) he explored in dramatic terms the consequences which arise from persons interpreting evidence mistakenly; he developed themes of jealousy and suspicion, although in these two plays he gave them a distinctly comic flavour. But it was to Ben Jonson's play *Every Man in His Humour* (1598) that Shakespeare may have turned for some of the details in *Othello*. Jonson's jealous merchant Thorello may have suggested Othello's name and indeed some of the traits of his character. For example, Thorello's denunciation of the pangs of jealousy that he suffers as a result of his wife Bianca's imagined adultery, anticipates very precisely the kind of problem that *Othello* explores in fuller tragic terms:

> First it begins
> Solely to work upon the fantasy,
> Filling her seat with such pestiferous air
> As soon corrupts the judgement; and from thence
> Sends like contagion to the memory,
> Still each of other catching the infection,
> Which as a searching vapour spreads itself
> Confusedly through every sensive part
> Till not a thought or motion in the mind
> Be free from the black poison of suspect.
> (*Every Man in His Humour*, I.4.203-12)

The context of *Othello*

Othello was first performed in 1604. Although it is the second of the so-called 'major tragedies' coming after *Hamlet* (1600-1), it seems to have much more in common with some of the earlier comedies, and certainly the subject of the cuckholded husband receives treatment in comedies right through to the Restoration. *Othello* is not a play about 'kingship', but rather about human passion. Its scope is, therefore, much narrower and more intense than that of *Hamlet*, or *Macbeth* (1606). It takes material that we usually associate with comedy, and explores its tragic possibilities.

This was not a new departure for Shakespeare. In some of his earlier plays he had attempted to deal alternatively with the comic and tragic implications of particular themes. For example, in *A Midsummer Night's Dream* (1595) he dramatised the comedy of thwarted love, but a year later *Romeo and Juliet* presented the tragic implications of this same theme. Similarly, in *Othello*, Shakespeare sought to examine the tragic implications of a series of themes to which he had already devoted some attention in earlier comedies. However, the intensity of the play's concern with extreme human passion and with 'evil' indicates a mood far from the exuberance of comic drama.

In *Hamlet* Shakespeare had dealt with the large political questions of 'kingship' and 'order'. In *Othello* he reduced considerably the scale of his artistic vision to focus upon more personal questions of 'judgement', and the extent to which human passion may be controlled. Othello is forced to choose between 'good' (embodied in the love that he shares with Desdemona), and 'evil' (embodied in Iago), but his powers of judgement become corrupted through Iago's villainy. Shakespeare shows us how the force of evil gradually asserts control over Othello's character, and how his noble mind falls prey to the very barbarism to which he has declared himself an enemy. The tragedy emerges from the paradoxes which this struggle generates, both internally in Othello's own mind, and externally in his relationships with other characters. The struggle ends in murder, but the hero finally manages to re-assert his former nobility and conquers the evil which has corrupted his mind. However, in Shakespearean tragedy generally, such a victory is always qualified. If the hero wins understanding of his character and destiny, then it is always at the expense of life itself. Othello's life is the price that he must pay for his understanding of how evil operates both in himself and, by implication, in the world generally.

The tragic philosophy of *Hamlet* in which Providence, the force which governs the conduct of human affairs, is shown working ultimately for the good of mankind, is modified considerably in *Othello*. In the later play Shakespeare considers the far less optimistic possibility that 'good' is constantly at the mercy of a universal 'evil'. We observe that at the end of the play it is Othello's life which is sacrificed—the 'good' in him dies along with the 'evil' he seeks to eliminate. His suicide restores to his character a measure of human dignity, but even so, Iago remains alive to signify the permanence of 'evil' as a force in the world. Shakespeare was drawn towards this view through his treatment of the darker, less easily explicable side of human nature in the so-called 'problem plays', *All's Well That Ends Well*, *Troilus and Cressida*, and *Measure For Measure*, which he wrote between 1600 and 1604. Indeed, in *Measure For Measure*, written probably just before *Othello*, the setting of the action is Venice, and the Duke Vincentio is the repository of Venetian law, working for the general good of his subjects in an atmosphere where uncontrollable sexual passion is a force to be reckoned with. It is Angelo, his deputy, to whom he entrusts the government of Venice during his contrived absence, and whose outward show of saintliness masks an inward devilish depravity, who is tested, thereby exposing a conflict between uncontrollable human passions and the Law which holds them in check. In this play the final balance, problematic though it turns out to be, is achieved in comic terms through a happy ending. In *Othello*, the focus shifts to the more sinister aspects of this human equation, developing and refining the dramatic treatment of evil itself.

The play offers us an insight into the ways in which Shakespeare refined and developed his own dramatic art. His choosing of the figure of a Moor for his hero was a stroke of brilliance. Othello's 'blackness' singles him out from the other characters in the play, but it would be quite wrong to infer from this that Shakespeare was concerned to depict some sort of crude 'racial' conflict. To the Elizabethans the figure of the Moor represented, not an ethnic but a moral type, and this partial view is presented in the play through the derogatory comments of Roderigo, Iago, and Brabantio. To them, the Moor epitomises lust, witchcraft, and satanic evil, all characteristics which were popularly associated with this 'type'. Shakespeare draws on these prejudices, but the play in no way supports them. Othello's physical appearance—his 'blackness'—serves to depict in vivid dramatic terms a *moral* challenge that the apparently civilised world of Venetian law believes it has overcome. Yet Othello is also the upholder of that law, a factor which should make us suspicious of any attempt to depict him as an 'outsider'. It is through this complex character that moral order and barbarism are made to confront each other symbolically, not in terms of a racial opposition, but rather in terms of the opposed moral forces which compete for supremacy in human nature itself.

To miss this point is to fail to understand the play's dramatic idiom. Moreover, our understanding of Shakespeare's method and technique in this play helps us to understand not only those plays which preceded it, but also the tragedies which followed: *King Lear* (1605), *Macbeth* (1606), and *Antony and Cleopatra* (1607).

A note on the text

As a professional dramatist Shakespeare's primary concern was to write plays for performance by actors whose skills he knew well. Consequently, he seems to have shown little personal inclination or concern to oversee the publication of his plays in book form, although there is some evidence to show that publication was occasionally sanctioned by the theatre company for which he worked. Even so, nearly half the plays which comprise the First Folio of 1623 had not appeared in print at all during his lifetime, while in the case of some (*Hamlet* and *Othello*, for example) the earlier quarto texts differ significantly from their Folio counterparts. Textual bibliographers have sought to account for these differences in a variety of ways, through the investigation of the peculiar habits of the printers who printed the plays, and through seeking to trace the original manuscript source which the printer may have used.

Othello is no exception to this general tendency. It was first published in quarto in 1622, some six years after Shakespeare's death, and eighteen years after its first appearance at the Globe. This text differs in some important details from that of the First Folio text which appeared a year later in 1623. Some critics have rejected the quarto text of 1622 as a corrupt version of the play, while others see it as the text which Shakespeare may have revised some time after its initial composition. It is argued that this revision, which adds a further 150 lines to the play, is the First Folio text of 1623.

The editor of the Arden edition of *Othello*, M.R. Ridley, chooses to rely more heavily for his text on the quarto of 1622 than most modern editors. His is perhaps the fullest and most informative readily available edition of the play, containing detailed notes, a good introduction, and the relevant passages from Cinthio's story which Shakespeare used as his main source. The line references in the glossary and in quotations from the play in these Notes are from this edition. Of the other editions available the New Swan Shakespeare edition, edited by Gamini Salgado is probably the most useful. Professor Salgado takes as his text the First Folio of 1623 but his introduction covers the wide range of issues which the play raises, and his annotations of the text are clear, accurate, and thorough. Kenneth Muir's New Penguin edition of the play, which also takes the 1623 First Folio as its text, is the least serviceable of the three, although it does contain a helpful critical introduction.

Part 2

Summaries
of OTHELLO

A general summary

Shakespeare's main concern in *Othello* is with the effects of jealousy upon the relationship between Othello and his wife, Desdemona. Their marriage is shown to be vulnerable from the start, since they appear to have eloped together, but the situation is made worse by the evil designs of the villainous Iago. Iago resents his having been overlooked for the post of lieutenant in Othello's army, and he is jealous of the success of his rival, Michael Cassio. As a way of gaining his revenge, he decides to 'poison' Othello's mind with lies about Desdemona's infidelity.

On the night of his marriage, Othello is called away to Cyprus, to defend it against possible attack from the Turks, and it is here, away from the security of Venice, that Iago hopes to put his plan into operation. His first plan is to disgrace Cassio, and then to use him to convince Othello that Desdemona has committed adultery with the fallen lieutenant. To this end he arranges a series of encounters designed to provide 'proof' of his allegations. Othello believes Iago, whom he thinks is 'honest', and after seeing Cassio with Desdemona's handkerchief, he is persuaded to change his attitude to his wife. He now thinks of her as a prostitute, and of himself as a disgraced and deceived husband. He decides to seek revenge for this indignity, and he murders Desdemona believing that her death is a just reward for the crime she has committed. But, after having killed her, an action which is irrevocable, he is made to realise the nature of the mistake he has made. When the full story of Iago's devilish plan is publicly revealed by her maid Emilia (Iago's wife), Othello seeks to recapture some of the nobility that he has lost, and kills himself.

Detailed summaries

Act I Scene 1

It is night in a street in Venice, and outside the house of a respected senator, Brabantio, two men, Iago and Roderigo are talking together. Though what they are discussing is not immediately clear, Roderigo appears dissatisfied with Iago's behaviour. Only later do we learn that the cause of his dissatisfaction arises from the secret marriage which has just taken place between Desdemona, Brabantio's only daughter, and the Moorish general, Othello. Iago appears to have been paid money to arrange a marriage between Roderigo and Desdemona, but his plan has failed, so he now tries to renew his partner's confidence in his competence and loyalty. He seeks to assure Roderigo of his hatred of Othello by revealing how he has himself recently been ignored for the post of lieutenant in favour of an inexperienced Florentine, Michael Cassio. Iago is utterly contemptuous of Cassio and says that his only reason for pretending to remain loyal to Othello is that sooner or later it will provide him with an opportunity to revenge this insult to his true worth and experience.

It appears that Brabantio does not know of his daughter's marriage to Othello, and so Iago urges Roderigo to' wake him and tell him. Roderigo obeys, and Brabantio appears only to hear a crude description of what has happened. The old senator does not at first believe what he hears. He responds by chiding Roderigo, thinking that he has come to pay court to Desdemona, and tells him that he does not consider him a suitable husband for her. Roderigo then explains in more courteous terms the purpose of his visit, and Brabantio is asked to go into his house to see if Desdemona is there. While he does so, Iago takes the opportunity to leave, claiming privately to Roderigo that he must now go and continue to pretend to be faithful to Othello. Brabantio returns, having verified Roderigo's story. On the basis of very little evidence he has accepted Roderigo's version of events and now goes to seek aid in searching for Desdemona.

NOTES AND GLOSSARY:

Tush, never tell me: Nonsense, you don't have to tell me
who hast my purse: to whom I have given money
this: refers to Othello's marriage
'Sblood: 'God's blood', a strong oath
three great ones of the city: three dignataries of the city of Venice
suit: to make an appeal to
Oft capp'd: showing respect
bombast circumstance: unnecessarily pompous language
Nonsuits: refuses to accept the appeal of
Forsooth: truly (but meant ironically)
damn'd in a fair wife: a sneer suggesting that Cassio's fondness for women will be his downfall
theoric: theory as opposed to practice
toged consuls: officials wearing togas, long-flowing garments worn by ancient Romans
lee'd and calm'd: becalmed as a sailing-ship at sea

debitor and creditor: an accountant

counter-caster: someone who counts with the aid of counters

ancient: 'ensign' or 'colour-sergeant', an army sergeant whose duty it is to look after the regimental flag. This is an appropriate title since Iago works throughout the play by means of 'signs'; 'ensign' means also 'to mark with a distinctive sign or badge'

letter and affection: a letter of recommendation, and irrational inclination

affin'd: compelled by duty

knee-crooking: someone who bows obsequiously

provender: to provide fodder for

cashier'd: dismissed from service

trimm'd . . . duty: whose outward appearance only indicates loyalty

lin'd their coats: feathered their nests, or prospered

figure: form

complement extern: outward appearance

I am not what I am: I am not what I appear to be

the thicklips: the first of a number of insulting references to Othello's Moorish origins

carry't thus: to succeed in conducting his affairs in this way

timorous accent: terrifying tone of voice

bags: money bags

Zounds: 'God's wounds', a blasphemous oath

black ram . . . grandsire of you: Iago describes the marriage crudely as a mating of two animals, and introduces the idea of Othello as a 'black devil'

distempering draughts: intoxicating drink, and hence drunk

grange: an isolated house

Barbary horse: Iago seeks here to combine the insulting suggestion of Othello as an animal, with that of him as an uncultivated barbarian

coursers: battle horses

gennets for germans: small Spanish horses for relatives

making . . . backs: consummating their marriage

odd-even: just after midnight

gondolier: a Venetian boatman

saucy: impertinent

tinder: the dry material used to kindle a fire

meet: appropriate or fitting

gall . . . check: injure his reputation with a reprimand

loud reason: the most obvious and reasonable choice

stands in act: are already under way

fathom: ability and experience

flag, and sign of love: Iago is referring here (ironically) to his role as 'ensign'
Sagittar: probably the name of the house where Othello and Desdemona are staying
charms: magic spells
discover: 'find' but also with the sense of 'uncover'
deserve: repay

Act I Scene 2

Meanwhile, Iago has arrived at Othello's house and has already begun to tell him of Brabantio's reaction to his marriage with Desdemona. His version of his own involvement in the events of the previous scene does not accord with what we already know, but Othello is in no position at this stage to be critical of Iago's account. Iago warns him that Brabantio may use his political influence to secure Desdemona's return, but Othello is confident that his own reputation and honour as a soldier will protect him from criticism. Someone is heard approaching. It is not the enraged Brabantio, but the newly appointed lieutenant, Michael Cassio. He has been searching for Othello with a message from the Duke of Venice summoning him to an urgent council meeting. Othello intends to obey the summons but leaves the stage for a moment, during which time the rivals Iago and Cassio converse briefly. Their conversation establishes Cassio's ignorance of Othello's marriage, and it also shows the extent to which Iago and Cassio differ in the ways they use language.

As Othello returns, Brabantio and his followers enter aggressively. Othello responds to this threat with power and authority, ordering them to sheath their weapons. They obey, but Brabantio now accuses Othello of having bewitched his daughter, and of stealing her, since he cannot believe that she would willingly agree to marry him. Othello remains dignified and aloof in the face of these insulting accusations, and says that he is quite prepared to answer them. Brabantio would prefer to see him imprisoned and brought to trial, but he is told that the Duke's urgent summons requires that he and Othello must attend the council meeting. Brabantio is surprised by this news, but as he leaves he insists upon the equal urgency of his own domestic problem.

NOTES AND GLOSSARY:
very stuff: essence or substance
I lack . . . service: I lack the villainy that would allow me to act selfishly
yerk'd: thrust
prated: prattled, or chattered childlishly

full hard forbear him: with some difficulty tolerate him

fast:	securely
magnifico:	a Venetian dignatory
a voice potential:	an influence as great
cable:	another of Iago's nautical metaphors, meaning 'scope'
signiory:	the Venetian council
out-tongue:	speak louder than
'tis yet to know:	it is not yet known
promulgate:	publish
siege:	literally 'seat', but meaning 'rank' or 'status'
unbonneted:	modestly and courteously
unhoused:	free, or unconfined

circumscription and confine: restriction and restraint

the sea's worth:	for all the sunken treasure in the sea
parts:	natural qualities
perfect soul:	fully prepared spirit
Janus:	the God with two faces: an appropriate oath for the 'two-faced' Iago
haste post-haste:	urgent
divine:	guess
heat:	urgency
sequent:	following each other
hotly:	urgently
about:	round the city
several:	separate
land carrack:	a large treasure ship. Iago here uses a metaphor of piracy
Marry:	an oath meaning 'by the Virgin Mary' but used here also as a pun on the verb 'to marry'
Ha' with you:	Let us go
I am for you:	you and I are equally matched opponents. But this is a pretence on Iago's part
enchanted:	bewitched with magic charms
refer . . . sense:	submit my argument to any normal examination

wealthy curled darlings: rich and attractive young Venetian men

guardage:	guardianship

judge me . . . sense: let the world judge how obvious my case is

weakens notion:	hinders any human response
disputed on:	debated
arts inhibited:	the forbidden arts of witchcraft
cue:	signal
prompter:	someone who reminds an actor of his lines when he has forgotten his part

course . . . session: due process of law
idle: trivial
actions . . . free: things may be allowed

Act I Scene 3

In the Venetian council chamber, the meeting to which Othello and Brabantio have been summoned is already under way. The enemies of Venice, the Turks, are about to launch a battle offensive, but their intentions are not yet clear. The Duke and his senators are faced with the problem of what might be done to resist this attack. The Duke analyses this problem wisely. He is obviously a careful ruler, who is not prepared (in contrast to Othello later) to make hasty judgements, and so we are confident that in all things he will act in a fair and just manner. Here we see him carefully weighing the evidence.

At the point when the Duke is certain that the Turkish fleet is travelling towards Cyprus, Othello and Brabantio enter with their followers. Both are welcomed by the council, but Brabantio immediately raises the issue of his daughter's marriage. What began as a meeting of the Venetian council to decide on a matter of political urgency, now becomes a legal trial in which Othello is accused of unlawfully marrying Desdemona. Othello is asked to explain his action, and he says that he is prepared to do so, but Brabantio, having now fully taken up the version of events suggested to him by Iago and Roderigo in the previous scene, repeats the accusation that his daughter has been the victim of witchcraft. As in the case of the activities of the Turkish fleet, the Duke is faced with a number of conflicting accounts, and he is asked to decide which is the correct one. Desdemona is summoned to appear, and while she is being brought to the council chamber Othello describes in detail his courtship of her. This convinces the Duke, and he tries to persuade Brabantio to accept the situation. Brabantio adamantly refuses, but now that Desdemona has arrived, he insists that she be allowed to give her version. She does so, supporting broadly what Othello had said before her arrival, and Brabantio agrees very reluctantly to withdraw his charges. The Duke, who is a humane man, tries to console Brabantio in the loss of his daughter, but he replies mischievously that if he must cheerfully accept this, then the Venetian government should equally cheerfully allow the Turks to capture Cyprus. This is an opportune moment to return to political matters, and the Duke does so, ordering Othello to go quickly to Cyprus, and allowing him to take Desdemona with him. Arrangements are made for Desdemona, who is to be placed in the charge of Iago whom Othello mistakenly believes to be honest. As they leave the Duke tries once more to console Brabantio, but he responds spitefully with a comment to Othello aimed at casting doubt on Desdemona's honesty. Although Othello dismisses this comment now, he recalls it to mind later in the play.

After the Duke and his council have left, only Iago and Roderigo remain, and they return to the question of Roderigo's hopes to marry Desdemona. Recent events now make it impossible for him to win her, but Iago persuades him that the marriage cannot last. At this point the play brings together the rejected suitor (Roderigo) and the cynical villain (Iago), simply in order to raise doubts about the security of the marriage between Othello and Desdemona. When Roderigo leaves, with renewed hope, Iago reveals in a soliloquy that his real objective is not to help his partner, but to revenge himself upon Othello for some past, and entirely unproven, insult.

NOTES AND GLOSSARY:

composition:	consistency
disproportion'd:	inconsistent
jump not:	do not coincide
aim reports:	offer approximate accounts
secure . . . error:	believe all the details
main . . . approve:	but I accept the gist of these reports
How say you:	What do you think of
assay:	test
pageant:	show
false gaze:	deceive us
importancy:	importance
with . . . it:	more easily capture it
brace:	readiness
dress'd in:	equipped with
wage:	risk
injointed . . . fleet:	united with a second fleet
re-stem:	retrace
frank:	true, or honest
servitor:	servant
free duty:	open respect
post post-haste:	speedy
lack'd:	were without
flood-gate:	pressing (like water against a flood-gate)
engluts:	swallows
mountebanks:	charlatan, or quack
err:	stray
Sans:	Without
beguil'd:	cheated
the bloody . . . sense:	you shall judge the case yourself, and impose without mercy the most extreme penalty

proper:	own
Stood . . . action:	Was the person you accused
mandate:	royal authority
potent:	powerful
head and front:	dimensions (but referring ironically to Othello's face, which is black.)
Rude:	rough, or uncultured
set phrase:	soft words
pith:	strength
nine moons:	nine months
tented field:	field of battle
feats of broil:	exploits in battle
grace:	add dignity to
round unvarnish'd:	plain unadorned
conjuration:	spell
motion:	impulse
maim'd:	crippled
vouch:	maintain
dram conjur'd:	potion strengthened with a magic spell
wrought:	worked
thin habits:	weak accusations
modern:	common
prefer:	allege
grave:	dignified
ran it through:	told it
moving accidents:	exciting misfortunes
th'imminent . . . breach:	at the very point of death
antres:	caves
idle:	empty
She'ld:	She would
pliant hour:	suitable opportunity
prayer . . . heart:	a serious promise
dilate:	tell at length
by parcel:	only in part
intentively:	continuously
beguile . . . tears:	coax tears from her
passing:	extremely
made . . . man:	created her as a man
bade:	implored
spake:	spoke
witness it:	testify to what I have said
mangled . . . best:	make the best of this imperfect affair
bad blame:	accusation
Light on:	descend upon

God bu'y:	God be with you
get:	engender
For your sake:	because of you
hang . . . 'em:	place heavy weights on their feet (to stop them from running away)
lay a sentence:	speak some wise words
grise:	step
late:	recently
takes:	removes it
Patience . . . makes:	Patient endurance helps us to withstand the loss
bootless:	to no avail
sugar:	make palatable, or agreeable
gall:	make bitter
equivocal:	capable of being understood in two ways
bruis'd . . . ear:	the wounded heart could be relieved by listening to the words of others
fortitude:	strength
allowed sufficiency:	proven ability
effects:	what must be done
slubber:	smear over
stubborn:	tough
boisterous:	violent
agnize:	acknowledge
A natural . . . alacrity:	an eagerness
bending . . . state:	with due deference to your dignity
fit disposition:	proper treatment
Due . . . place:	treatment according to her status
exhibition:	provision
besort:	suitable companions
As . . . breeding:	according to her background
my unfolding:	what I am about to say
charter:	permission
trumpet:	publish
visage:	face (Desdemona says here that she judges Othello's character by his inner qualities—his mind—and not by the colour of his face)
consecrate:	dedicate
a moth of peace:	useless and idle
bereft:	taken from
heavy interim:	sorrowful time
support:	endure
heat:	lust
affects:	passions
scant:	neglect

In . . . satisfaction: this is a corrupt line, but modern editors agree that Othello is saying that he will not allow physical desire to rule him, but that he is attracted above all to Desdemona's spiritual qualities

light-wing'd toys: trivial matters

feather'd Cupid: the arrow of Cupid, the Greek God of Love

speculative . . . instruments: my physical and mental powers

disports: pleasures

skillet: saucepan

helm: helmet

indign: unworthy

make head against: attack

honesty: integrity (This is the first use of this term in relation to Iago)

conveyance: trust

delighted: delightful

quick: alert

best advantage: at the most opportune time

incontinently: forthwith

prescription: a doctor's advice

guinea-hen: prostitute

hyssop: an aromatic herb

unbitted: unbridled

sect: cutting

perdurable: long-lasting

stead: help

defeat thy favour: disguise your appearance

usurp'd: false

sequestration: separation

acerb: bitter

coloquintida: a bitter apple used as a purgative

sated: fed up

erring: sinful

out of the way: not the correct way to proceed

fast: stick firm

hearted: vigorous

cuckold him: deceive him by seducing his wife

betimes: early

profane: devalue

expend: spend

snipe: fool

twixt . . . office: seduced my wife (Iago has no evidence for this accusation, but this does not prevent him from acting as though it were true)

surety:	certain
smooth dispose:	cultivated manner
engender'd:	born

Act II Scene 1

The action now moves from Venice to Cyprus (and remains there for the rest of the play) where both Othello's generalship and his marriage with Desdemona will be subjected to thorough testing. Here far from the safety and stability of Venice, Iago intends to carry out his devilish plan of revenge, which will seek to undermine Othello's own moral defences against the threat of evil. Montano, the governor of Cyprus whom Othello is coming to replace, and two other men anxiously await Othello's arrival. Because a storm is raging, they cannot see which ships are approaching, and so they have to guess what is happening. This recalls the uncertainty which we noticed at the opening of the previous scene, and which in different ways is emphasised throughout the rest of the play.

News arrives that the Turkish fleet has been scattered in the storm, but that Othello's lieutenant, Cassio, has arrived safely in Cyprus. Othello's own safety still remains in doubt, but we do get a brief glimpse, in what Montano says, of the esteem in which he holds the new governor. His point of view contrasts greatly from that which Iago holds about Othello's character. Cassio enters and reassures Montano that Othello's ship is strong enough to withstand the storm, and in the meantime news arrives that a ship has been sighted. Before this ship docks Cassio has time to confirm the rumour that Montano has heard of Othello's marriage, and he praises Desdemona's virtues. Immediately afterwards Desdemona, Iago, Emilia, and Roderigo arrive, having disembarked from the ship which has just docked, and both the ladies are welcomed courteously by Cassio. There is further news of a second ship having been sighted, but all (including the audience) are forced to wait in suspense before knowing for certain that it carries Othello. Desdemona tries to suppress her fears for her husband's safety by passing the time in light-hearted conversation with Iago, although the subject of their discussion, the characters of women, will prove to have direct relevance to Iago's plots later in the play. Iago cynically devalues women, accusing them of hypocrisy, deception, and wantonness, and he even goes so far as to suggest that they are naturally inclined towards evil deeds. Desdemona defends women against Iago's criticisms, but while she turns for a moment to speak with Cassio, he reveals in an 'aside' to the audience that he will transform their innocent gestures of courtesy into evidence to support his allegations of Desdemona's dishonesty.

It is only after the threat of Turkish invasion has been dispelled, and after these alternative views of human behaviour have been established, that Othello finally steps ashore. Ironically, there are new dangers facing him, of which he is not yet aware. Desdemona's courteous welcome of her husband is counterbalanced by Iago's private reminder to the audience that this happiness will be short-lived. All then leave for the castle, save Iago and Roderigo who remain to discuss the first stages of Iago's plan. Roderigo is fooled throughout into helping Iago, and he is persuaded here into thinking that Cassio's courteous gestures of welcome to Desdemona indicate that they are secretly in love with each other. Thus, if Roderigo wishes to secure Desdemona for himself, he must first discredit Cassio. Roderigo leaves after having agreed to find a way to provoke Cassio to lose his temper in public, leaving Iago on stage to remind us of his continued hatred for Othello. The plot against Cassio will allow him to take his revenge on two enemies at once, although his reasons for wanting to do so are far from clear.

NOTES AND GLOSSARY:

high-wrought flood:	extremely rough sea
main:	the sea
descry:	see
ha' ruffian'd so:	has raged so
mountains:	mountainous waves
mortise:	wood-joints
segregation:	scattering
banning shore:	the shore which repels the advance of the waves
chiding billow:	noisy waves
surge:	swelling of the waves
main:	bulk
burning bear:	the star called the Little Bear
guards . . . pole:	the stars in the same constellation as the Little Bear, known as the Guardians, both used as aids to navigation
like molestation:	such a disturbance
enchafed:	angry
enshelter'd, and embay'd:	sheltered and harboured
bear it out:	withstand it
designment:	plan of attack
halts:	made lame
grievous . . . damage:	a severe damage and wrecking of
Veronesa:	a ship fitted out at Verona (alternatively it may mean a 'cutter')
Touching:	concerning

sadly:	gravely
Even . . . regard:	Until we make the sea and the sky indistinguishable from each other
elements:	the wind and the waves
Is . . . well-shipp'd:	Is his ship well-built?
bark:	ship
stoutly:	strongly
approved allowance:	proven reputation
not surfeited:	not excessive
bold cure:	in good health
My . . . for:	I hope it is
discharge . . . courtesy:	fire a shot (salvo) to signal friendship
wiv'd:	married
paragons:	surpasses
excels . . . pens:	exceeds poetic descriptions of her
And . . . excellency:	And excels in outward beauty
put in:	landed
gutter'd:	jagged
ensteep'd:	under-water
guiltless:	innocent (important in its application to Desdemona's ship)
footing:	arrival
se'nnight's:	week's
extincted:	extinguished
Enwheel:	Encircle
contention:	conflict
citadel:	fortress
gall . . . patience:	make you impatient
extend . . . manners:	proffer a courteous welcome
You'ld:	You would
ha' list to:	want to
chides . . . thinking:	is silently critical
Bells:	Noisy
housewives:	hussies
Turk:	infidel (ironically, the values which Iago upholds show him to be a 'Turk'—an attacker of the Venetian way of life)
put me to't:	force me into it
critical:	censorious, apt to find fault
assay:	try
I am . . . otherwise:	I am sad, but I am trying to hide my sadness by appearing to be happy (this is an innocent deceit of the kind that Iago will use against Desdemona later)

about it:	thinking about it
pate:	brain
birdlime:	a sticky substance used to catch birds
frieze:	woollen material (hence Iago is saying that he finds it difficult to think, but the metaphor he uses is one of ensnaring)
deliver'd:	delivered of (compare this metaphor with that of 'birth' which Iago uses at I.3.402)
wit:	mental alertness
paradoxes:	attitudes not commonly held
pranks:	wanton actions
did . . . itself:	could justifiably claim the approval of malice itself
cods . . . tail:	make a foolish exchange
wight:	person
chronicle . . . beer:	take note of trivial things
profane:	outspoken
liberal:	bawdy
home:	plainly
clyster-pipes:	douches
Olympus-high:	as high as Mount Olympus
If . . . die:	If I were to die now
set . . . pegs:	slacken the strings so as to produce a discord
As . . . am:	For all my apparent honesty
prattle . . . fashion:	speak carelessly
coffers:	luggage
challenge . . . respect:	requires that we respect him
presently:	immediately
list me:	listen to me
Lay . . . thus:	place your finger on your lips and listen
act of sport:	sexual activity
give satiety:	satisfy it
begin . . . gorge:	to be sick of it
pregnant:	natural
conscionable:	conscientious
salt:	bawdy
has . . . themselves:	is able to make opportunities which would not have arisen by themselves
green minds:	inexperience
fig's end:	the term for an obscene gesture made either by biting one's own thumb, or by thrusting the thumb between both forefingers
paddle:	stroke
marshal:	show
incorporate:	combined (that is, their bodies come together)

tainting . . . discipline:	upsetting his self-control
minister:	provide
in choler:	to anger
qualification:	agreement to remain at peace
displanting:	uprooting
prefer:	advance
apt . . . credit:	fitting and plausible (here again Iago 'creates' facts without having any firm evidence for them)
peradventure:	perhaps
accountant:	accountable
diet:	feed
seat:	bed
inwards:	insides
That . . . cure:	That he will lose his powers of judgement
I trash:	I hold in check
stand . . . on:	will withstand my holding him in check
on the hip:	will throw him like a wrestler (and therefore will have him at my mercy)
rank garb:	coarse manner
with . . . too:	will usurp my bed also (another of Iago's unproven accusations)
egregiously an ass:	a complete fool
practising:	plotting
Knavery's:	Villainy's

Act II Scene 2

In this brief scene a herald announces that both the destruction of the Turkish fleet and the consummation of Othello's marriage (which, because of the urgency of his mission, has not yet taken place) are now to be celebrated. These celebrations will be allowed to continue into part of the night. Ironically, the freedom which Othello generously extends to his followers will become the very licence which Iago takes to disrupt the festivities. Thus this proclamation, while indicating the passage of time and a return to order, also provides the opportunity for villainy, and will enable Iago to disturb the peace in every way (as he had done with Brabantio in I.1.)

NOTES AND GLOSSARY:

mere perdition:	complete destruction
offices:	kitchens (for the supply of food and drink)
told:	struck

Act II Scene 3

After having arrived at the castle, Othello and Desdemona make preparations for their private wedding celebration. Othello warns Cassio to take care that the public festivities, which are already under way, do not get out of hand, and his lieutenant assures him, without the slightest awareness of any irony, that Iago has everything under control. Othello and Desdemona leave just as 'honest' Iago arrives.

Cassio wants immediately to attend to the duties that he and Iago have been entrusted to carry out, but is persuaded that there is still a little time left for celebration. He and Iago discuss, from two very different viewpoints, the virtues of Desdemona, with Iago constantly emphasising in a lewd way, her physical attributes, and he then asks Cassio to drink some more wine with him. Cassio reluctantly agrees, and goes out briefly to call in some of his companions. This gives Iago the opportunity to present to the audience his plan for making Cassio drunk and quarrelsome, thereby endangering the newly-won peace in Cyprus. The unsuspecting Cassio returns with Montano and some others, and the celebration begins. Cassio is plied with wine, and is soon drunk, but as he leaves asserting his sobriety, Roderigo approaches and is urged by Iago to follow the lieutenant. Having set this plot in motion, Iago now turns to Montano and tells him in confidence that Cassio's qualities as a soldier are marred by his habitual drunkenness. Montano is surprised at this revelation, and thinks that Othello should be told, but he has no time to question the truth of it before Roderigo returns, being driven in by an angry and drunken Cassio. Montano appears convinced, and is wounded when he interferes to stop the quarrel. Meanwhile the alarm bell is sounded, summoning Othello from his marriage-bed. After having cunningly engineered this disturbance, Iago now assumes the role of peacemaker, while Othello orders that the bell be silenced and begins to question all concerned. Cassio and Montano say nothing, and so the explanation is left to Iago, who, with some show of reluctance reveals that it was Cassio who began the quarrel. He describes the situation using the metaphor of a 'bride and groom' who begin by intending to celebrate their wedding, but end in disagreement, thus keeping before us the main objective of his plot to corrupt Othello's love for Desdemona. For this lapse Cassio is dismissed from his post as lieutenant. At this point Desdemona enters, emphasising by her very presence the consequences of this disturbance. Thus Shakespeare brings on to the stage all of the [unknowing] participants in the plot which Iago has secretly devised. Having dispensed a summary justice, Othello leaves with Desdemona, and only Cassio and Iago remain. It is now Cassio's turn to be manipulated, in the same way as Roderigo had been earlier. He is utterly dejected at the loss of his reputation, but Iago urges him to ask Desdemona to plead with Othello on his behalf. Cassio agrees, and leaves believing (like Othello himself) that Iago is, indeed, honest. Iago now turns to the audience claiming that the advice he has given Cassio is reasonable, but he goes on to say that this is part of the more general deception he practises, and that the next stage in the plot must be to convince Othello that Desdemona's appeals arise from the 'fact' that she is secretly in love with Cassio. Roderigo now returns, beaten and dejected, more doubtful than ever that he will succeed in securing Desdemona. But just as the dejected Cassio has been given some hope, so Roderigo is counselled to be patient, and as morning approaches he is sent away more sanguine about his future. Iago has now to put the finishing touches to his plan by securing the unwitting help of his wife Emilia in ingratiating Cassio with Desdemona.

NOTES AND GLOSSARY:

honourable stop:	decent restraint
outsport discretion:	go beyond the limits
with . . . earliest:	as soon as you can
fruits . . . ensue:	our marriage is not yet consummated
this hour:	for another hour
cast us:	dismissed us
blame:	censure, or criticise
made . . . night:	spent the night (Iago regards the consummation of their marriage in disparagingly physical terms)
full of game:	expert in love-making
parley of provocation:	provokes lusty thoughts
alarm:	signal for the pursuit of
stoup:	a tankard or jug
without:	outside
brace:	pair
fain . . . measure:	would like to drink
I'll . . . you:	I will drink more than my share (and thus help you)
qualified:	diluted
innovation:	change
fasten:	persuade him to drink
carous'd:	drunk
Potations . . . deep:	drink to the bottom of his tankard
honour . . . distance:	are very ready to take offence
elements:	types
consequence . . . dream:	to judge by the way my plot is developing
stream:	current
a rouse:	a draught
cannikin:	small tankard
potent . . . potting:	expert in drinking

swag-bellied Hollander: fat Dutchman
with facility: easily
Almain: German
gives . . . vomit: makes a Dutchman sick
pottle: tankard
do . . . justice: drink as much as you
peer: nobleman
breeches: trousers
held: considered
lown: rascal
wight: person
owd: old
set . . . watch: mount the guard
stand . . . Caesar: act as Caesar's right-hand man
give direction: issue orders
a just equinox: an exact counterbalance
on . . . infirmity: at a time when his illness (that is, his drunkeness) is at its height
evermore: always
prologue . . . sleep: before he goes to sleep
horologue: clock
double set: twice round
Praises: Evaluates
ingraft infirmity: inbred disease
wicker bottle: a bottle encased in basket-work
prate: prattle
mazzard: head
mutiny: riot
Diablo: the Devil
rise: wake up
carve: strike a blow
motion: action
propriety: quietness
In quarter: in the positions assigned to them
terms: circumstances
Devesting: Undressing
unwitted . . . men: as if some planetary influence had driven men mad
tilting: thrusting
peevish odds: foolish quarrel
to . . . it: to become a part of it
you . . . forgot: you forgot yourself
wont: inclined
stillness: sobriety
mouths . . . censure: is spoken by those who are wise in judgement

unlace:	undo
rich opinion:	the high opinion others have of you
to danger:	dangerously
spare . . . me:	do not talk because it hurts me to do so
aught:	anything
amiss:	wrongly
self-charity:	kindness to myself
assails:	attacks
collied:	blackened (This is a prophetic claim and shows that Othello's own powers of judgement can become blackened by irrational passion. He is unaware at this stage of the irony of his remark.)
rebuke:	censure
foul rout:	disgraceful brawl
set it on:	provoked it
approv'd:	proven guilty
twinn'd . . . birth:	had been my twin
manage:	engage in
partially affin'd:	committed
leagu'd . . . office:	connected by official position
Touch . . . near:	Do not examine too closely something which affects me deeply (Iago says this fully aware of its irony)
nothing . . . wrong:	will not wrongly accuse him
determin'd . . . him:	his sword drawn determined to strike him
entreats . . . pause:	begs him to stop
Outran . . . purpose:	Ran too fast for me to catch him
high . . . oaths:	shouting abuse
I . . . before:	I had never seen before
mince:	mix
light:	favourable
sweeting:	darling
hurts:	injuries
balmy:	soothing
recover:	regain the love of
cast . . . mood:	dismissed because of his anger
in policy:	calculated
malice:	enmity
offenceless:	innocent
affright:	scare
imperious:	majestic
sue:	importune
speak parrot:	talk nonsense
discourse fustain:	argue bombastically
nothing wherefore:	no reason for it

moraler:	moraliser
befallen:	happened
Hydra:	the many-headed monster whom Hercules had to kill (in the Greek legend.)
unordinate:	excessive
ingredience:	contents
familiar:	friendly
mark:	study
denotement:	noting
parts:	qualities
splinter:	to put into splints, and hence to knit together
lay:	bet
betimes:	early
undertake:	intercede
check:	hold in restraint
Probal to thinking:	Open to approval
fram'd:	built
fruitful:	generous
free elements:	the elements of earth, air, fire and water
infetter'd:	enslaved
list:	wants
appetite:	his desire for her
weak function:	natural inclinations
parallel:	coinciding with my purpose
repeals:	wants him reinstated
enmesh:	entrap
fills . . . cry:	one who merely makes a noise, but who does not lead in the hunt
cudgel'd:	beaten
wit:	awareness
by . . . witchcraft:	by intellect and not by magic
dilatory time:	taking time
cashier'd:	dismissed from service
billeted:	stationed
move:	intercede for
set . . . on:	persuade her to do it
jump:	at the precise time
device:	design or plot

Act III Scene 1

It is now morning, and Cassio has engaged a troupe of musicians to serenade Othello and Desdemona, according to Venetian custom. Othello, however, seems not to have liked the music and sends a bawdy

Clown to pay the musicians to leave. Cassio takes this opportunity to ask the Clown to convey a message to Desdemona's lady-in-waiting, Emilia, and the latter agrees. As the Clown goes off, Iago makes a timely entrance (notice he always arrives in time to assist with the progress of his plots) and he agrees to help Cassio by diverting Othello, so that he may speak the more freely with Desdemona. Meanwhile, Emilia has received Cassio's message and comes to tell him that Desdemona has already begun to intercede with Othello on his behalf, and that he may shortly be reinstated. We should remember that although Iago said in the last scene (II.3.373) that Emilia was to be persuaded to put Cassio's case to Desdemona, it is clear from what happens subsequently that he did not intend to approach her directly on the matter himself. Thus, when Emilia tells Cassio that she will take him to speak personally with Desdemona, she has no idea of the part she is playing in the plot which Iago has contrived.

NOTES AND GLOSSARY:

content your pains:	reward your labours
instruments:	musical instruments (but the Clown intends a bawdy pun)
Naples:	The Clown may be alluding here to 'the Neapolitan disease' or the pox
speaks . . . nose:	smell
tail:	genitals (the musician mistakes the Clown's meaning and assumes that 'tail' means 'story')
quillets:	quibbles
entreats:	begs
In happy time:	you have come at an opportune moment (again Cassio is unaware of the irony of his remark)
a-bed:	to bed
a mean:	a plan
great affinity:	of noble rank
safest occasion:	best opportunity
bring you in:	reinstate you
bestow:	place
bosom:	heart
much bound:	indebted

Act III Scene 2

We return now to Othello who is concerned with military matters. He proposes, probably in accordance with Iago's plot to divert his attention, to inspect the fortifications of the town. The deep irony of this scene lies in the fact that while he is inspecting the defences against attack from the outside, he is unwittingly involved in a plot which is already under way to undermine his own domestic security from within.

NOTES AND GLOSSARY:
do:	convey
works:	fortifications
Repair:	Return

Act III Scene 3

This is the central scene of the play towards which all of Iago's plotting has been directed. Still believing Iago to be sincere in his concern for Cassio, Desdemona and Emilia assure the fallen lieutenant that all will be well between him and Othello. We hear this conversation in its entirety in order that we may savour the full irony of the interpretation that Iago will place upon it later. Cassio secures a promise from Desdemona to be persistent on his behalf, but on seeing Othello and Iago approaching, he declines her invitation to stay and leaves. His motive for doing so is the shame he feels for his recent indiscipline, but Iago does not miss this opportunity to suggest to Othello that his leaving may have another, less respectable significance. Iago is questioned further about this, but he is very evasive in his replies, allowing suspicion of Cassio to implant itself gradually in Othello's mind. It is in this mood of uneasiness that Othello encounters Desdemona who begins immediately to sue for Cassio's reinstatement. Her earnestness serves only to add fuel to his growing suspicion and his off-hand replies to her suggest that he already has doubts about her honesty. Desdemona and Emilia leave, but the doubt that Othello feels forces him at this crucial point to re-emphasise his love for his wife in truly cosmic terms. For him she is the embodiment of the principle of 'order', but it is this very principle which is already threatened. Iago sees his chance, and gently infers that the recent conversation between Cassio and Desdemona may have been less respectable than it might have appeared at first sight. Othello is eager to know more, but Iago's hesitant replies are carefully designed to convey the impression that the truth is more sordid than he feels it proper to utter. Othello takes the bait and his suspicions grow, fed carefully by Iago with his pointed comments about the natural inclination of women to deceive their husbands. It is at this moment that he chooses to revive Othello's memory of Brabantio's warning. Thus he moves slowly to the point where he can counsel Othello to resist the temptation to be jealous, a suggestion designed to have precisely the opposite effect of encouraging feelings of jealousy. Iago carefully prepares a point of view from which Othello cannot help but observe Desdemona's and Cassio's actions, thereby contaminating beforehand any judgement which he might subsequently pass on them. Othello has now to arbitrate between the conflicting evidence of his knowledge of his wife, and the reports which Iago has carefully constructed, and the result is a growing doubt in a mind where there was previously only certainty and trust. We are only made aware of the full extent of the damage that Iago has done in Othello's first soliloquy of the play, in which he tries to find reasons for his wife's infidelity even before he has had the chance to prove it. Here he seems to have taken over Iago's cynical view of human nature completely, but when Desdemona returns, his mind becomes confused again. The purpose of her return is to remind him of an official duty which he has (contrary to his earlier promise to the Duke of Venice) neglected to perform, but she notices immediately a disturbing change in her husband's manner. In her efforts to comfort him she accidentally drops her handkerchief, which had been Othello's first present to her. After they have left, Emilia picks it up and on Iago's return gives it to him. When Iago is alone he reveals that he will now place the handkerchief in Cassio's lodgings, to be found there as evidence of his secret affair with Desdemona. Othello now returns almost completely convinced of Desdemona's guilt, but demanding certain proof of it. Iago continues cautiously to feed his jealousy and suggests that final proof might be obtained by asking Desdemona to produce the handkerchief. With this prospect of positive proof in sight, Othello now turns his thoughts to revenge. With characteristic irony, Iago promises his help, and after they have planned Cassio's death they leave, with Othello declaring that Iago is to be his new lieutenant.

NOTES AND GLOSSARY:

All . . . abilities: All I possibly can

I know . . . his: in claiming that Iago's concern for Cassio is considerable, Emilia is being more ironic than she realises

strangest: strangeness

politic: expedient

policy: contrivance

nice: trivial

breed . . . circumstance: grow to the point where opportunity is lost

supplied: filled

warrant: guarantee

article: detail

watch . . . tame: prevent him from sleeping, and hence make him tame

shrift: confessional

do . . . discretion: do as you think best

present:	immediate
in cunning:	intentionally
prithee:	I pray you
faith:	in faith
trespass:	offence
in . . . reason:	according to what we think normally
check:	rebuke
mammering:	hesitating
bring . . . in:	reinstate him
boon:	something asked as a favour
entreat:	implore
peculiar profit:	particular benefit
poise:	weight
beseech:	beg
straight:	directly
Perdition:	Damnation
Chaos . . . again:	Disorder is returned
between us:	acted as an intermediary (Iago pounces on the ambiguity of this statement)
of . . . counsel:	confidentially aware
purse:	knit
conceit:	idea
stops:	hesitations
tricks . . . custom:	customary devices
close denotements:	secret indications
that:	what (it is ironical since we already know what Iago thinks about this: see II.3.342)
would . . . none:	I wish they would not appear to be men
Certain:	Certainly
as . . . thinkings:	what are your thoughts
ruminate:	consider (them) in your mind
free to:	free from
As where's:	Where there is, for example
whereinto:	into which
uncleanly apprehensions:	unwholesome interpretations
leets . . . law-days:	days on which local courts of justice meet
conspire:	plot
makest . . . thoughts:	do not allow him access to your thoughts
vicious . . . guess:	malicious in my interpretation
jealousy:	suspicion
You'ld:	That you would
scattering:	haphazard
quiet:	peace of mind
Good name:	Reputation

filches:	steals (This entire speech is ironical since Iago has already stolen Cassio's reputation)
not . . . him:	does not make him richer
mock:	ridicule
cuckold:	the husband of a wife who has committed adultery
tells:	counts
fineless:	endless
I'ld:	I would
exsufflicate:	inflated
blown:	blown up
franker:	more outspoken (It is Iago's apparent 'frankness' that Othello and others applaud as 'honesty'. In this scene we see how wrong they are)
Wear . . . thus:	Look like this
self-bounty:	natural generosity
country disposition:	native inclination
best conscience:	sense of morality
seal:	sew up
close . . . oak:	as close together as the grain found in oak
bound . . . ever:	indebted to you for ever
dash'd:	smashed
grosser:	more lewd
vile success:	evil consequences
affect:	desire
matches:	marriages
clime . . . degree:	country, colour, and status
Whereto:	To which point
tends:	inclines
rank:	foul
in position:	as part of my exposition
recoiling . . . judgement:	going back upon her own judgement
match . . . forms:	compare you with the appearance of her own countrymen
happily:	perhaps
scan:	examine
fills . . . up:	occupies it
strain . . . entertainment:	exaggerates her pleas on his behalf
busy . . . fears:	too occupied in my suspicions
government:	judgement
all qualities:	all human characteristics
human dealing:	experience
haggard:	wild (that is, not properly trained) hawk
jesses:	leather straps attached to a hawk's feet
down . . . wind:	with the wind behind it

prey . . . fortune:	to survive as best she may
soft . . . conversation:	social graces
chamberers:	courtiers, that is, ladies' men
vale of years:	approaching late middle age
abus'd:	deceived
delicate:	refined
vapour:	air
Prerogativ'd . . . base:	They are more vulnerable than those of humble birth
unshunnable:	unavoidable
forked plague:	the sign of the cuckold's horns
quicken:	are born
generous:	noble
napkin:	handkerchief
remembrance:	keepsake
wayward:	capricious
conjur'd:	solemnly instructed
ta'en out:	copied
fantasy:	whim
to the advantage:	luckily
Be . . . on't:	Remain ignorant of it
conceits:	imaginings
mines . . . sulphur:	hell fire
poppy:	opium
mandragora:	a soporific drug
drowsy syrups:	sleep-inducing medicines
owest:	had
Avaunt:	Be off with you
wanting:	desiring
Pioners:	lowest rank of soldier
plumed:	glorious
trump:	trumpet
mortal engines:	deadly cannon
counterfeit:	imitate
occupation:	vocation
ocular:	visual
probation:	proof
hinge . . . loop:	a hook and eye on which something might be hung
amaz'd:	horrified
God buy you:	God be with you
that:	what
Dian's:	Diana the Roman godess of chastity
suffocating streams:	streams which drown (possibly strams of volcanic lava)

put . . . you:	told you about it
supervisor:	spectator
topp'd:	seduced
prospect:	situation
bolster:	in bed together
prime:	lusty
hot:	lecherous
salt:	lecherous
imputation . . . circumstance:	opinion and strong circumstantial evidence
living:	valid
office:	duty
sith:	since
raging tooth:	toothache
gripe:	grasp
foregone conclusion:	something which has already taken place
shrewd doubt:	ominous suspicion
thicken:	strengthen
fond:	foolish
hearted throne:	throne in men's hearts
fraught:	freight or burden
aspics' tongues:	tongues of poisonous snakes
content:	calm
Pontic Sea:	The Black Sea
compulsive:	relentless
Propontic:	Sea of Marmora
Hellespont:	Dardanelles
capable:	comprehensive
yond marble:	yonder marble-like in its hardness
clip:	surround

Act III Scene 4

After a climatic ending to the previous scene, this one begins light-heartedly with Desdemona asking the Clown of Cassio's whereabouts. But, beneath the surface wit of the Clown's replies, lies the more sinister practice of insinuating the wrong meanings into words, thereby perverting language generally, and making it difficult for Desdemona to extract from him the information she requires. The Clown is dismissed and Desdemona begins to search for her handkerchief. Othello enters, now thoroughly convinced of his wife's guilt, and managing only with some difficulty to be courteous to her. He takes her hand in his, but claims that this gesture which was once a token of affection has now lost all meaning, and then he asks for the handkerchief. Desdemona hesitates, but is told of its magical properties; thus from being an insignificant 'napkin' too small to use in comforting Othello in the previous scene, it has now grown to a symbol of wedded love, the loss of which will provide proof of Desdemona's infidelity.

Under a pressure with which we can readily sympathise, Desdemona lies in saying that it is not lost, and tries to change the subject to that of Cassio's reinstatement. This simply intensifies Othello's anger, and he storms out demanding to see the handkerchief. Emilia, who in this scene is given the task of commenting on the action, sees that Othello is jealous. Iago and Cassio approach, and after having been told of Othello's change of manner, Iago goes out, ostensibly to find what has caused it.

Desdemona is herself upset and confused by what has happened, and after a brief conversation with Cassio she too leaves. While Cassio is waiting for her to return, his mistress Bianca enters and chides him for not having visited her recently. He gives her the handkerchief and has to explain, in the face of her suspicions, that he found it in his lodgings. He wants to have it copied, and after promising to visit her soon, they leave.

NOTES AND GLOSSARY:

lies:	(line 1) stays
lies:	(line 2) tells a lie (the Clown alternates between the two meanings of the word throughout this dialogue)
edified:	enlightened
catechize:	question
within . . . compass:	within the ability
crusadoes:	gold coins stamped with a cross
humours:	moods
dissemble:	pretend
moist:	moist as a sign of lust (but Desdemona responds— as she had done in the dialogue with the Clown —to its alternative meaning, that of indicating youthfulness)
fruitfulness:	generosity, but also amorousness (as with the word 'moist')
liberal:	free, but also licentious
sequester:	restraint
castigation:	correction
excercise:	act of worship
heraldry:	emblem
chuck:	a term of endearment
salt . . . rheum:	bad cold
charmer:	someone skilled in magic

amiable:	desirable
hold:	consider her to be
loathly:	disgusting
wive:	marry
perdition:	complete destruction
sibyl:	prophetess
that . . . compasses:	who is two hundred years old
fury:	frenzy
mummy:	liquid derived from embalmed human bodies and used as a magic potion
skilful:	those skilled in magical arts
Conserve . . . hearts:	Preserved from maidens' hearts
startingly:	in a disgusting manner
an if:	if
misgives:	makes me suspect
hungerly:	hungrily
purpos'd . . . futurity:	the merit I intend to get in the future
must . . . benefit:	will do me more good than uncertainty
forc'd:	reluctantly accepted
shut . . . alms:	pursue my fortunes in some other way
blank:	target
blown . . . ranks:	shot his soldiers to pieces
Puff'd:	Blown up
moment:	importance
unhatch'd practice:	prematurely discovered plot
demonstrable:	apparent
puddled:	clouded
wrangle:	find fault with
object:	target
indue:	lead to
observances:	attentions
bridal:	wedding day
unhandsome:	unbecoming
suborn'd:	wrongfully procured
What . . . home?:	What are you doing here?
leaden:	heavy
strike . . . absence:	pay the debt I owe you for being absent
Take . . . out:	Copy for me
Go to:	Away with you!
ere:	before
addition:	credit to me
woman'd:	subdued
bring . . . little:	go with me some of the way
circumstanc'd:	yield to circumstances

Act IV Scene 1

This scene begins, as did the opening scene of the play, in the middle of a conversation. Just as Roderigo had been duped by Iago earlier, so now Othello is fooled, as he is cautiously reminded by his new lieutenant of what Desdemona may have given Cassio. Because her honour is something that is invisible, its absence cannot be proved, but the missing handkerchief is evidence of an altogether more substantial nature. Othello begins by hovering uneasily between Iago's version of events, and his knowledge of Desdemona, but once Iago begins to exploit language (significantly playing upon the meaning of the word 'lie') Othello's defences crumble and he collapses on the ground paralysed. As Iago gloats over his conquest, Cassio enters and shows concern for Othello, but when he begins to recover from his fit, Iago instructs Cassio to leave but to meet him later. Othello now wants more proof, and Iago devises a plot to provide it by having him overlook a conversation with Cassio. Othello withdraws and Iago outlines the plot in more detail as Cassio makes a timely return. In the conversation that follows, Othello only sees Cassio's gestures, but does not hear all of what is being said, and therefore misinterprets its meaning completely. The subject of the conversation is, in fact, Cassio's mistress Bianca, but Othello believes that it is Desdemona. Even when an enraged Bianca storms in brandishing the handkerchief that Cassio gave her, Othello sees only what Iago wants him to. When Bianca and Cassio have left, he comes from hiding, more convinced of his wife's dishonesty and Cassio's guilt, and determines that both shall die. Iago conveniently suggests that Desdemona should be strangled in bed, and agrees to arrange the murder of Cassio himself. At the very point at which Othello commits himself finally to Iago's point of view, news arrives from Venice that he is to be recalled, and that Cassio is to govern Cyprus in his place. The Venetian ambassador Lodovico, who knows Othello only as a noble general, now witnesses his degradation of Desdemona as she is beaten and unceremoniously dismissed from Othello's presence. He is shocked at this behaviour, and bewildered as Othello storms off inarticulate with rage. Ironically, it is Iago to whom he turns for an explanation, and he regrets that the confidence of the Venetian government in Othello should have been so misplaced. Thus, even at the point when Othello publicly commits himself to evil, we are tactfully reminded of his former nobility.

NOTES AND GLOSSARY:

unauthoriz'd: unlawful

hypocrisy . . . devil: hypocrisy to cheat the Devil (that is, by threatening to commit a sin, but finally not doing so)

yet . . . so:	lie naked in bed together
So:	If
venial slip:	pardonable misdemeanour
essence:	essential quality
They . . . it:	They seem to have it
Boding:	Threatening disaster
importunate suit:	ardent wooing
dotage:	weakness
Convinced . . . supplied:	Satisfied their lust
blab:	brag
unswear:	deny
Lie:	Iago plays on the two meanings of the word here as did the Clown in III.4)
belie:	slander
fulsome:	foul
invest:	dress
instruction:	intimation of positive proof
credulous:	naïve
dames:	women
reproach:	disgrace
forbear:	stop
lethargy:	fit
straight:	straight away
great occasion:	some important matter
Would . . . would:	O that you would
horned man:	a husband deceived and dishonoured by his wife's adultery, who wears two horns on his head as a sign that he has been cuckolded
yok'd:	married
draw . . . you:	join you
unproper:	not belonging to them
dare . . . peculiar:	claim to be theirs alone
arch-mock:	supreme joke
lip:	kiss
secure:	free from care
patient list:	within the bounds of patience
shifted . . . away:	fobbed him off or attempted to satisfy with an excuse or pretence
extasy:	fit
encave:	hide
cope:	seduce
all . . . spleen:	completely ruled by passion
cunning:	skilful
keep . . . all:	keep control above all

housewife:	prostitute
unbookish:	untutored
conster:	interpret
addition:	title
speed:	be successful
caitiff:	wretch
laughs . . . out:	laughs it off
Roman:	perhaps refers to the triumphal marches of victorious Roman generals
customer:	prostitute
bear . . . wit:	be more charitable to my intelligence
cry:	rumour
scor'd:	access to information about my future (it may also mean 'wounded' since Iago can claim credit on both counts)
flattery:	self-flattery
haunts me:	follows me persistently
bauble:	worthless thing
hales:	draws attention to
Before me!:	My goodness!
fitchew:	polecat
hobby-horse:	prostitute
An:	If
rail:	rant
very fain:	very much like to
prizes:	values
have . . . a-killing:	spend nine years torturing him to death
gentle . . . condition:	so kind a nature (Iago plays on its alternative meanings 'yielding' or 'pliant')
fond over:	dote on
patent:	permission
messes:	pieces
expostulate:	debate
unprovide:	weaken
undertaker:	provider
instrument . . . pleasures:	the means whereby they command me (that is, the letter Lodovico has brought)
atone:	reconcile them
make . . . amends:	apologise to her
crocodile:	false (as the tears of the crocodile)
turn:	(line 248) return (line 249) lie on her back like a prostitute (Othello exploits the two meanings of this word)
well-painted:	well-counterfeited

anon:	shortly
shot . . . chance:	danger or bad fortune
light . . . brain:	mad
censure:	critical opinion
Is . . . use?:	Is this what he usually does?
courses:	ways of behaving

Act IV Scene 2

Othello, still determined to confirm Desdemona's guilt, now questions her lady-in-waiting, Emilia. She can offer him no evidence to justify his suspicions, but while she is sent to fetch Desdemona Othello dismisses her testimony, thereby violating the principle of listening to both sides of the story before passing judgement. Emilia returns with Desdemona, but is then dismissed, leaving Othello to question her privately. Desdemona understands neither the purpose or meaning of her husband's enquiry, and continues to protest her innocence. This frustrates Othello even further, revealing a growing obsession with his own newly-discovered significance as a model for all cuckolds; he responds by turning everything Desdemona says in her own defence against her, using Iago's now familiar method of exploiting the alternative meanings of particular words. When Emilia returns, she finds her mistress treated as a prostitute, and her own position transformed into that of a procuress. Othello's onslaught leaves Desdemona stunned and speechless, and she asks, with some difficulty, that Iago be summoned. He appears and pretends ignorance to the cause of Othello's behaviour; Emilia attempts to find an explanation, and accidentally stumbles on what we know to be part of the truth, but Iago dismisses her suggestion as improbable. He offers an alternative explanation, that Othello may be disturbed by his military responsibilities, and eager to take any opportunity to change the subject, urges the two women to go in to supper. Emilia's speculation, apart from countering Iago's earlier suspicion of Othello, is the nearest that her husband's plots have come to being publicly exposed. Iago now faces another challenge from a distinctly unhappy Roderigo who enters demanding to know what he has done with the jewels and money he has received. Roderigo's threat to approach Desdemona directly, endangers Iago's position, but the latter responds by drawing his victim into the plot to kill Cassio. By the time they leave Roderigo is thoroughly persuaded by Iago's explanation, but demands to know more about the plot.

NOTES AND GLOSSARY:
breath . . . up:	said
durst:	dare

Lay . . . stake:	Lay down my soul as a wager
requite:	repay
serpent's curse:	the curse that God placed on Satan in the Garden of Eden
simple bawd:	naïve procuress or madam of a brothel
A . . . key:	the lock and key of a private room (guarding her mistress's secrets)
Some . . . function:	Go about your business as a bawd
procreants:	those about to procreate
cry hem:	clear your throat as a sign of warning
mystery:	trade
dispatch:	get on with it
one of heaven:	angel
occasion:	reason
your . . . back:	calling you back (to Venice)
lost him:	lost his favour
try . . . affliction:	test me with suffering
Steep'd:	Buried
fixed figure:	permanent example (as the figure on a clock face)
slow moving:	the hands on the clock which move so slowly that they appear to be still
garner'd:	stored
fountain:	source or spring
current:	life-blood
cistern:	pool
gender:	procreate
Turn . . . complexion:	Turn your fair face
cherubin:	angel (Othello seems here to be comparing his black face with that of Desdemona)
shambles:	slaughterhouse
quicken:	come to life
blowing:	laying their eggs
committed:	(line 72) done (line 74) committed adultery? (Othello is exploiting the alternative meanings of the word)
very forges:	red as the fire from a blacksmith's forge
stops . . . nose:	holds its nose
hollow mine:	cave
strumpet:	whore
vessel:	body
Saint Peter:	the guardian of the gates of heaven
turn . . . key:	lock the door after me
keep . . . counsel:	keep our affair secret
go . . . water:	tears
meet:	fitting

opinion:	criticism
abuse:	fault
chid:	chided
bewhor'd:	accused of being a whore
despite:	abuse
callat:	slut
Beshrew:	Curse
trick:	deception
insinuating:	twisting his way into favour
cogging, cozening:	cheating and conniving
halter:	noose
companions:	villains
unfold:	reveal
squire:	rogue
seamy . . . without:	inside out
discourse . . . thought:	thinking
them:	themselves
shake . . . off:	discard me
forswear:	disown
abhors me:	disgusts me
addition:	label
does . . . offence:	worries him
stay:	wait on you
justly:	fairly
doffest:	fobs me off
conveniency:	wellbeing
than:	rather than
put . . . peace:	peacefully tolerate
no kin:	not related
wasted . . . means:	squandered all my money
votarist:	a nun
aquittance:	requittal, or repayment for a debt
fopp'd:	made a fool of
give over:	give up
intendment:	intention
mettle:	spirit
devise . . . for:	contrive ways of taking
compass:	- the bounds of possibility
abode:	stay
linger'd:	postponed
determinate:	effective
harlot:	prostitute
fashion:	arrange
fall out:	happen

Act IV Scene 3

After supper, Lodovico, the Venetian ambassador, invites Othello to go for a walk, and he agrees but orders Desdemona to go to bed. Alone, Emilia helps Desdemona to prepare, and she is critical of Othello's recent behaviour. Despite the treatment she has received, Desdemona continues to be loyal to her husband, but the strain of having to withstand such abuse makes her mind wander to thoughts of death, and to a song which she cannot forget. This song was first sung by her mother's maid, Barbary, who had also received similar treatment from her lover; its recall at this precise moment serves to reinforce the sadness of Desdemona's own plight. After having sung the song, Desdemona begins to question Emilia about whether women capable of the deception of which she has been accused actually exist. Emilia, who is both realistic and worldly, says that they do, and tries, perhaps rather cynically, to make light of Desdemona's desperate situation by placing her alleged crime in a different perspective. Women, she argues, are unfaithful usually in response to the deficiencies of their husbands. The view she expresses is completely opposite to that of the relationship between man and woman that Iago offered to Desdemona earlier in the play (II.1). Desdemona is sceptical that an evil deed is justified as a response to another evil deed, and says that she prefers to learn the ways of the world through suffering. This short scene, full of foreboding, serves to keep firmly before us the magnitude of Othello's error. It is also the last opportunity Desdemona has to consider her own values before they are tested by means of the suffering to which she refers.

NOTES AND GLOSSARY:

o' the instant:	quickly
dispatch:	dismiss
incontinent:	immediately
approve:	approve of
checks:	rebukes
All's one:	It doesn't matter
I . . . do:	I can hardly avoid
barefoot . . . Palestine:	made a pilgrimage to Palestine
nether:	lower
willow:	symbol of unhappiness in love
hie:	hurry
moe:	more
couch:	sleep
gross kind:	crude way
by . . . light:	by the moon (Emilia twists Desdemona's meaning in her reply)

joint-ring:	ring with two separable halves
measures:	lengths
lawn:	linen
exhibition:	reward
venture purgatory:	risk the torments of hell
for . . . labour:	for what you have done
to . . . vantage:	more than that
store:	populate
slack:	relax
scant . . . despite:	reduce our allowances out of malice
galls:	the ability to be resentful
affection:	inclination
usage:	'habit' or perhaps 'treatment'

Act V Scene 1

While Desdemona is preparing for bed, and unwittingly for her own death, Iago and Roderigo prepare to murder Cassio. Up to this point in the play Iago's perverse interpretation of motive and event has led only to Cassio's loss of his reputation, but to no irreversible action. The murder he now plans, and later, the murder of Desdemona, are designed to trap both Roderigo and Othello into actions from which there can be no escape. After instructing Roderigo, Iago reveals to the audience that it would be convenient if both Cassio and his gullible assailant were to kill each other. As Cassio comes walking by in the darkness he manages to avoid Roderigo's half-hearted attack, but is wounded by Iago. He calls desperately for help and Othello enters, briefly gloating in the mistaken belief that the murder of Cassio has gone according to plan, and goes off with renewed confidence to carry out his revenge on Desdemona. Cassio's cries also draw Lodovico and Gratiano who approach cautiously, believing that this may be some sort of trap. Only when the hypocritical Iago comes back with a lantern do they come nearer. While they are attending Cassio, Roderigo, who had himself been wounded in the attack, cries out for help, but Iago goes over and stabs him, thereby eliminating the threat that he might pose at some future time. The noise has also attracted Bianca, but when she comes to investigate, she is immediately accused by Iago of having had some part in the assault on Cassio. A brief search reveals the dead body of Roderigo, and Iago now begins to insinuate that he may have quarrelled with Cassio over Bianca. The last person to arrive on the scene is Emilia (whose opinion of human nature we already know) and she is told that Cassio's injury is the result of his lechery. With characteristic opportunism, Iago now sets about implicating Bianca further, and demands to know Cassio's movements in the time prior to the assault. When it is established that he had been with Bianca, Emilia turns on her abusively. Though she defends her honour, and though there is really no hard evidence to implicate her, Bianca is taken away, while Emilia is instructed to inform Othello and Desdemona about what has happened. Iago's brief aside to the audience at the end of the scene reiterates the importance of the events of this night in relation to the overall success of his plan, and serves to sustain to the end an atmosphere of extreme tension.

NOTES AND GLOSSARY:

bulk:	shop-front
mars:	spoils
devotion to:	enthusiasm for
quat:	pimple
to . . . sense:	until it hurts
makes . . . game:	serves my purpose
calls me:	will want from me
restitution:	settlement
bobb'd:	swindled
unfold me:	discover me
make proof:	test
hies apace:	hurries on
passage?:	no one passing?
mischance:	misfortune
very direful:	one of extreme distress
come into:	come nearer to
cries on:	cries out
spoil'd:	badly injured
make away:	escape
prove:	approve
garter:	some material to bind a wound with
trash:	rubbish (referring to Bianca)
bear . . . part:	be involved
cry you:	I beg your
accidents:	misfortunes
Save . . . labour:	Stop what you are doing (that is, tending Cassio's wound)
malice:	ill-will
out . . . air:	indoors
an . . . stir:	you may well be disturbed
anon:	shortly
'Las:	Alas
charge:	order
dress'd:	have his wound attended to

tell's:	tell us
happ'd:	happened
foredoes:	ruins

Act V Scene 2

Believing that Cassio is already dead, Othello now stands over the sleeping Desdemona. Like Iago, he carries a lantern, but his intention to violate their marriage-bed associates him ironically with darkness and not with light, with evil and not with justice. He proceeds to outline in soliloquy his justification for the act he is about to commit, but even though he is ironically convinced of its rightfulness, he is disturbed by the fact that once he kills Desdemona, he will not be able to bring her back to life again. The contrast between Desdemona's physical beauty, and what Iago has persuaded him is her inner corruption, still moves him, and he laments the paradoxical and tragic situation in which he now finds himself, of having to kill the woman he loves. When Desdemona awakes, he asks her directly to pray for her soul, a request which distinguishes him from a more traditional revenger like Hamlet, since his primary concern is to seek to eradicate the sins of her body. Desdemona is frightened and vulnerable in her innocence, but Othello returns to the topic of the handkerchief. She denies having given it to Cassio, but when she asks that he be summoned to corroborate her story, Othello reveals that he has already been murdered. Othello's position here is highly ironical since we know that Desdemona did not give Cassio her handkerchief, nor indeed has he been murdered. The helpless Desdemona is now smothered, while outside Emilia is knocking, with information which might well have saved her, but because of his concern over the act he has just committed Othello does not answer immediately. When he does finally unlock the door to let her in she gives him the news that Cassio is not dead but that Roderigo is. The few final words of vindication which the dying Desdemona utters draws Emilia's attention to another, more horrifying death, the tragic dimensions of which have yet to emerge. Desdemona dies reiterating her own innocence, and in a last, and characteristically magnanimous gesture of selfless love, absolves Othello from responsibility for her death. The shocked Emilia now begins to question Othello and to assert Desdemona's innocence in the face of an action which she is convinced is devilish. Slowly the truth about Iago emerges, but when she realises it her hesitations (unlike those of Iago in III.3) reflect a genuine horror of what has happened, and she screams for help. Montano, Gratiano, and Iago come rushing in, and for the first time in the play Iago is confronted publicly with the knowledge of his evil schemes. A shocked Gratiano reveals that had not Desdemona's father, Brabantio, died of grief, this spectacle would have forced him to deny that there was any goodness in human nature. Iago, now keenly aware that his own position is threatened, tries to silence Emilia, but she reveals exactly how Desdemona's handkerchief came to be in Iago's possession, thereby corroborating the dead woman's story. Othello, himself aware that this investigation is taking place too late, strikes Iago who responds by stabbing Emilia and running off. Divested of his former glory by the knowledge of his tragic mistake, and completely wretched, Othello, the once noble warrior, is easily disarmed, while Montano and Gratiano hurry out in search of Iago. Meanwhile, Emilia in a re-enactment of Desdemona's death, recalls her mistress's 'willow' song and dies reasserting her innocence. Lodovico, Montano, and the injured Cassio enter with Iago whom Othello now wounds in an attempt to kill him. In complete bewilderment he demands an explanation for Iago's villainy but Iago, so adept at persuasion, resolves to remain stubbornly silent. Cassio's evidence confirms the truth of Desdemona's story, and he reveals also that a letter has come to light implicating Iago and Roderigo in the plot on his life. Lodovico in his role as Venetian ambassador relieves Othello of his command, and hands the government of Cyprus over to Cassio. It is at this moment, after Othello has come to realise the magnitude of his own crime, that he recalls to mind his own former commitment to the defence of Venice against the Turks. He seeks now to place his crime in a context which all are invited to approve, a context which is inclusive, and one in which Othello can define publicly the part that he has been persuaded to play. His story of the 'Turk' who overcame a Venetian and undermined the security of the state of Venice, is clearly applicable to his present situation. The reminder of his former nobility forces him to enact upon himself the very sentence he had passed upon the Turk. Thus he pursues to a tragic conclusion the logic which had caused him to kill Desdemona, and in seeking to redeem his own soul from evil, and to reassert his nobility, he commits suicide. The loss of Othello's life is balanced by the dignity and honour he redeems for himself by his final action, and we are left both with a sense of final justice and of waste at his death. While Othello and Desdemona lie dead upon their marriage-bed, Lodovico now turns his attention to Iago, who has caused the tragedy. The play ends with him being led off to be tortured in an effort to loosen his tongue, while the ambassador promises to carry the story of Othello's tragic fall back with him to Venice.

NOTES AND GLOSSARY:

cause:	reason
light:	Othello plays with two meanings here: (*a*) the light he is carrying (*b*) Desdemona's life

quench:	put out
minister:	agent
cunning pattern:	skilful product
Promethean:	Prometheus, in Greek legend, stole the fire from the Gods and brought it down to earth
relume:	rekindle
balmy:	soothing
Justice . . . sword:	Justice was usually depicted as a woman blindfolded, who carried a sword in one hand and scales in the other
So . . . fatal:	Nothing so attractive as this could be so deadly
bethink yourself:	think of
Unreconcil'd . . . heaven:	for which you have not yet obtained heaven's forgiveness
Solicit:	Ask for pardon
walk by:	stand aside
forfend:	forbid
knaw:	bite
nether:	lower
frame:	body
so . . . matter?:	but tell me what is wrong?
perjury:	lying on oath
conceit:	conviction
withal:	with
warranty:	allowance
stone . . . heart:	hardened your heart
ta'en order:	made arrangements
interprets:	makes me believe
had stomach:	had an appetite
strive:	struggle
like:	likely
it:	there
yawn . . . alteration:	gape as in an earthquake
error:	wandering out of its orbit
out of tune:	not in harmony (with Othello's plans for revenge)
harsh:	discordant
belie:	slander
top:	mount
else:	if you do not believe me
were:	would be
But:	Except
extremity:	extreme
chrysolite:	topaz (semi-precious stone)
slime:	dirt

iteration:	repetition (contrast Iago's 'iterations' in III.3, designed to deceive Othello)
made . . . with:	made a mockery of
pernicious:	villainous
half . . . grain:	that is the smallest part
you . . . best:	you had better (be silent)
gull:	fool
apt:	plausible
charm . . . tongue:	be quiet (Iago's success up to this point has depended upon his ability to persuade others not to question his plans publicly)
proper:	fitting
Perchance:	Perhaps
mortal . . . him:	killed him
Shore . . . atwain:	Severed the strands of his life (probably a reference to Atropos (one of the three Fates in Greek legend) cutting the threads of human life with her shears)
do . . . turn:	do something desperate
better angel:	that is his good angel
reprobation:	damnation
act . . . shame:	adultery
works:	endeavours
recognizance:	acknowledgement
pledge . . . love:	that is, the handkerchief
antique:	very old
dull:	stupid
speak'st on:	are talking about
fortune:	accident
coxcomb:	idiot
stones:	thunderbolts
Precious:	Arrant or downright
puny whipster:	weak hothead
Let . . . all:	Let it all go
bode:	foretell
play . . . swan:	the swan was thought to sing only before its death
bliss:	paradise
ice-brook'd temper:	tempered in ice-cold water
perforce:	necessarily
your stop:	the hindrance which you present
weapon'd:	armed
butt:	objective
sea-mark:	direction
lost:	groundless
Man . . . rush:	Brandish even a reed

ill-starred wench:	unfortunate woman (this is the literal meaning of the name Desdemona)
smock:	night-dress
at count:	at the Day of Judgement
steep-down:	precipitous, with sides as steep as precipices
viper:	poisonous snake (referring to Iago)
towards . . . feet:	that is to see if he has cloven hooves like the Devil
Wring:	Take
in my sense:	according to the way I feel
wert:	was
Fall'n practice:	Fallen victim to the plots
ensnar'd:	trapped
thou . . . best:	you do well (that is, to remain silent)
befall'n:	happened
imports:	concerns
undertook:	carried out
discontented:	full of discontent
belike:	more than likely
nick:	in the meantime
satisfied:	that is killed
wrought . . . desire:	fashioned in accordance with his plot
upbraids:	holds to account
Brave me:	Provoke me
cast:	dismissed from office
taken off:	removed
hold him long:	prolong his agony
close:	shut up
Soft you:	Wait a moment
extenuate:	mitigate
aught:	anything
wrought:	manipulated
Perplex'd:	Confused
melting mood:	crying
Set . . . down:	Write this down
medicinal gum:	myrrh
malignant:	rebellious
traduc'd:	betrayed
smote:	struck
period:	ending
marr'd:	spoiled
Spartan dog:	vicious animal
fell:	fierce
keep:	guard
censure:	judgement

Part 3

Commentary

Othello is a play about deception and revenge, and to this extent it shares certain similarities with the tragedy which immediately precedes it, *Hamlet*. In the earlier play the hero, envious of 'that man/That is not passion's slave,' (III.2.68-9), learns to control his passion and moves towards a rational outlook which will enable him to revenge the death of his father. Othello, however, is persuaded by Iago to *relinquish* his control of passion (and along with it his 'honour' and powers of rational judgement) in order to revenge a wrong which has not actually been committed.

There are one or two further distinctions to be made between the two plays. At the level of plot, the dramatic conflict in *Hamlet* is between the 'mighty opposites' Hamlet and Claudius, each seeking to outwit the other, and thereby initiating actions which comprise the structure of the play. By contrast in *Othello*, the entire plot, and its conduct, are in the hands of the villain Iago. His intricate plans which involve the duping of Roderigo, the 'poisoning' of Brabantio's mind, the discrediting of Cassio, and finally the deaths of Desdemona and Othello, are all directed towards the destruction of the hero himself. Othello's compliance with Iago's plots is undertaken without his knowledge of their true objective, and to some extent this lessens the burden of responsibility which we feel he should bear. That he does finally assume that responsibility elevates him to the status of tragic hero.

Themes

The major themes in *Othello*, the various connecting ideas which give unity to the dramatic action, are bold and striking. The critic A.C. Bradley, in his book *Shakespearean Tragedy* (1904), has observed that the atmosphere of the play resembles that of 'a close-shut murderous room', indicating the sheer intensity of the action. Indeed, the most cursory reading of the play reveals an absence of direct concern with the wider issues of 'kingship' or 'the Elizabethan world picture' in the sense that we encounter them in the history plays, or in either *Hamlet* or *Macbeth*. Even though Othello murders Desdemona at night (darkness being a pervasive feature of the play), his action fails to arouse a response from Nature in the way that, say, Macbeth's murder of King Duncan does:

Methinks it should be now a huge eclipse
Of sun and moon, and that the affrighted globe
Should yawn at alteration.

(V.2.100-2)

It is as though Nature's refusal to respond serves to underline the supreme tragic irony of Othello's position at this point since the 'cause' to which he has dedicated himself, and which he discusses at the opening of the final scene of the play (V.2.1-6) has no basis in reality whatever. He has been persuaded into believing that all women are false, and that Desdemona's physical appearance is evidence of her duplicity. What follows is based upon Othello's acceptance of these two dubious assumptions.

Throughout the play we are aware of the discrepancy between what particular characters appear to be, and what they are. This conflict between 'appearance' and 'reality', so pervasive in Shakespeare's plays generally, opens out in *Othello* into the wider moral perspective of the conflict between 'good' and 'evil', in which nearly all the central characters, with the notable exception of Iago, are unwittingly caught up. It is Iago who provides the key to this intense and elemental conflict, and his frank admission to the foolish Roderigo in the opening scene of the play serves as a principle which guides the action towards its tragic conclusion:

For when my outward action does demonstrate
The native act, and figure of my heart,
In complement extern, 'tis not long after,
But I will wear my heart upon my sleeve
For doves to peck at: I am not what I am.

(I.1.61-5)

This conflict of appearance and reality which the play keeps before us, extends also, in an unusual way, to Othello himself. Ironically, up to the point where Iago persuades him otherwise (III.3.205ff.) he assumes that outward appearance and action is a clear reflection of human personality. When counselled by Iago to hide himself from Brabantio's anger, Othello responds with:

Not I, I must be found:
My parts, my title, and my perfect soul,
Shall manifest me rightly:

(I.2.30-2)

Later, though by this time a little less certain, he asserts: 'Certain, men should be what they seem.' (III.3.130-2). But, throughout, Othello's own *appearance* raises some doubts about the validity of this assumption. His 'perfect soul' is not openly reflected in his face which is, of course, black. As if to lend support to this anomaly, Iago's evil is not reflected in the 'honesty' of his face. By direct contrast, Desdemona is both 'perfect' in her soul, and 'fair' in her outward appearance. When asked about her marriage to Othello, her reasons echo the general principle which he has already declared; her perception of the qualities of Othello's mind informs her sense of his visual appearance:

I saw Othello's visage in his mind,
And to his honours, and his valiant parts
Do I my soul and fortunes consecrate:
(I.3.252–4)

Of course, Iago is aware of the weak foundation of this principle, especially since Othello is the literal *embodiment* of its possible contradictions. And it is this distinction between appearance and reality which he uses to suggest that there is some substance in the allegation that Desdemona is false.

As Othello becomes more suspicious, so he begins to lose the self-possession which was a feature of his behaviour in Act I. When he finds that others may not be what they seem, he begins to reflect on his own deficiencies, and as he does so he becomes more aware of his own physical appearance:

Haply for I am black,
And have not those soft parts of conversation
That chamberers have, or for I am declin'd
Into the vale of years—
(III.3.267–70)

Later he seeks to give his own 'blackness' an emblematic value, as a physical reflection of what he believes is his sullied reputation: 'my name, that was as fresh/As Dian's visage, is now begrim'd and black/As mine own face:' (III.3.392–4). This is an attempt to find a measure of consistency amid contradictions. So conscious is Othello of the gulf between appearance and reality that he laments the passage of old customs, and their replacement with others which cannot guarantee certainty; as he takes Desdemona's hand he observes: 'the hearts of old gave hands,/But our new heraldry is hands not hearts.' (III.4.42–3). This leads finally to his own analysis of the contradictions which he believes she embodies: 'O thou black weed, why art so lovely fair?' (IV.2.69).

Othello's analysis, however, is not allowed to stand alone. Desdemona does not embody these contradictions, nor is she concerned to draw meaning from Othello's own physical appearance. For her, his 'blackness' is of no significance at all, since she sees his 'visage in his mind' (I.3.252) and holds this view consistently throughout the play. For

Emilia, who enters and sees Desdemona lying dead, Othello's 'blackness' is an outward sign of the devilish nature of his action: 'O the more angel she,/And you the blacker devil!' (V.2.131–2). Finally, for us, and for the play as a whole, Othello's 'blackness' carries yet another, perhaps more complex meaning. He is the tragic hero of the play, and black, the colour which Elizabethans normally associated with stage tragedy, is therefore a fitting symbol of his status. Thus, at the heart of the play lies an intricate and vividly dramatic emblem, the meaning of which changes as the action moves forward. At the outset the epithets 'Noble Moor' and 'black devil' vie with each other for supremacy, as we try to evaluate Othello's character. They give way in the middle of the play to his own view of himself as a cuckold (he sees himself at IV.2.75ff., in a striking image, as Vulcan, the blacksmith of the Gods, whose wife Venus committed adultery with Mars), but culminates finally in his establishment as tragic hero taking full responsibility for his mistaken action, and combining these opposites in a new and impressive dramatic unity. Thus, the play ends with a restoration of continuity, achieved at the expense of Desdemona's and Othello's deaths, in which appearance and reality can now be openly distinguished from each other.

Setting

The action is divided between Venice and Cyprus, and moves from the centre of civilised behaviour in Act I, to the hostile environment of Cyprus for the remainder of the play, where the marriage of Desdemona and Othello will be tested. In this respect, the play resembles one of the earlier comedies, *As You Like It* (1598–9) in which the action moves from the Court (whose values differ somewhat from those of Venice in *Othello*) to the Forest of Arden where the characters undergo a series of rigorous tests of their ideas and beliefs. In Shakespeare's plays generally particular locations are usually endowed with symbolic meaning, especially when we remember that on the Elizabethan stage the absence of scenery suggests that dramatists were not concerned to reproduce the physical characteristics of a particular place for their own sake. Bearing this in mind, what values do Venice and Cyprus represent in the play, and what do they contribute to our understanding of the central dramatic conflict? Let us look firstly at Venice.

When Iago and Roderigo waken Brabantio in the opening scene of the play, he responds in the following manner:

What, tell'st thou me of robbing? this is Venice,
My house is not a grange.

(I.1.105–6)

Brabantio's surprise indicates that robbery and law-breaking in Venice are unusual. Even after having established to his limited satisfaction that Iago's and Roderigo's story has some truth in it, he goes to confront Othello with the Venetian law: 'To prison, till fit time/Of law,' and course of direct session,/Call thee to answer.' (I.2.85-7). In the scene which follows this confrontation we observe the workings of Venetian law at two levels. Firstly, the Duke of Venice, in whose authority the law is vested, has to deal with an external threat to the stability and peace of Venice. But he methodically gathers evidence from his advisers, weighs different possibilities, and only sanctions action when he is certain of the direction in which the enemy fleet is travelling. Secondly, he deals with the internal problem of Brabantio's intemperate accusations, but he uses the same method, allowing both Othello and Desdemona to speak before deciding on a course of action. That the Duke is persuaded by Othello's story is vital in establishing the hero's worth according to the standards of Venice:

> If virtue no delighted beauty lack,
> Your son-in-law is far more fair than black.
> (I.3.289-90)

But Shakespeare deliberately introduces a certain precariousness into the situation since he wishes to demonstrate how, in particular circumstances, these standards can be made vulnerable to attack. In Venice, at any rate, the more cynical view of human nature which Iago and Roderigo express, and to which Brabantio, and later Othello, fall prey, is held firmly in check by the judicious judgement of the Duke. It is upon this foundation that Othello's 'reputation' rests, a point which receives an unexpectedly dramatic emphasis later in the play when the shocked ambassador, Lodovico, watches him abuse his wife in public:

> Is this the noble Moor, whom our full senate
> Call all in all sufficient? This the noble nature,
> Whom passion could not shake? Whose solid virtue
> The shot of accident, nor dart of chance,
> Could neither graze nor pierce?
> (IV.1.260-4)

It is in Cyprus, at the very point where Venetian and 'Turk' meet, that the standards established in the opening act of the play are to be tested. The precarious Venetian hold on Cyprus reflects a psychological battle waged in and around the character of Othello himself, as Iago begins to undermine his authority and judgement. The stormy uncertainty of Desdemona's and Othello's arrival in Cyprus, and the tenuous victory over the Turkish fleet (which in strict terms is not exactly a victory), lends atmosphere to the moral uncertainties to come. The tension is maintained since Cyprus is in a state of military readiness, in need of defence, and demanding alertness and judgement from its defenders.

The first major weakness in the Venetian defence (which is, of course, the prologue to the exposure of a more serious weakness) occurs when the drunken Cassio forgets himself and threatens the security of the citadel. His violation of the standards of 'courtesy' and 'duty' expected of him is recognised by Othello himself, who places Cassio's indiscretion in a larger, more prophetic context:

> Are we turn'd Turks, and to ourselves do that
> Which heaven has forbid to Ottomites?
> For Christian shame, put by this barbarous brawl;
> (II.3.161-3)

This disturbance not only threatens the safety of the town: 'What, in a town of war,/Yet wild, the people's hearts brim full of fear,' (II.3.204-5), but it also challenges Othello's own self-control: 'Now by heaven/My blood begins my safer guides to rule,' (II.3.195-6). This precarious psychological balance, reflecting as it does, the equilibrium which was maintained in Venice, is exactly what Iago intends to upset. Thus, what is respectable in Venice, loses its respectability in Cyprus; the virtuous Desdemona is transformed into a common Venetian housewife who, according to Iago, habitually deceives her husband:

> I know our country disposition well;
> In Venice they do let God see the pranks
> They dare not show their husbands: their best conscience
> Is not to leave undone, but keep unknown.
> (III.3.205-8)

Cassio's loss of self-control, directly attributable to the drink foisted upon him by Iago, has an important parallel to Othello's relinquishment of his 'safer guides', as he falls prey to a feeling of suspicion which has its origin in the same source. The issues which the brawl raises reappear, in a slightly different guise at the end of the play, at the point where the now fallen Othello fights with himself to reassert control:

> And say besides, that in Aleppo once,
> Where a malignant and a turban'd Turk
> Beat a Venetian, and traduc'd the state,
> I took by the throat the circumcised dog
> And smote him thus.
> (V.2.352-6)

The psychological conflict which he acts out at the end of the play is reflected in the conflict between Venice and Cyprus, the Venetian and the Turk, civilisation and barbarity, which is central to the action and meaning of the play.

Character and characterisation

We have already observed the intensity of Shakespeare's dramatic vision in *Othello*, and some of the ways in which the central psychological conflict is given wider scope and meaning. It is not surprising, given Shakespeare's impressive grasp of the complexities of human affairs, that the characters he draws should engage our attention as full individuals, of the kind that we sometimes find in novels. On the other hand, to react too strongly against this, as critics sometimes do, and to view particular characters as moral 'types', for example Desdemona as 'good', or Iago as 'evil', is to fail to give full credit to Shakespeare's considerable powers of dramatic characterisation. Desdemona is 'divine', but she has married without her father's consent, and she is, as her name suggests, 'ill-fated'; similarly, although Bianca's name means 'white', she is considered by Iago and Emilia to be a prostitute. Clearly, the general question of characterisation in Shakespeare's plays is fraught with dangers which admit of no easy solution. Perhaps one way of unlocking the full dramatic ambiguity of Shakespeare's characters is to consider their individuality in relation to their function as contributors to the action which the playwright seeks to present. Thus, while it would be wrong to see them purely as 'devices', moral or otherwise which the dramatist uses as part of his overall technique, it would be equally wrong to think of them as 'people' in the everyday sense of the term. To press beyond the limits which the play lays down, is to risk isolating the characters from the carefully integrated structure which gives them life and meaning. Bearing this significant, but difficult reservation in mind, let us now look more closely at the characters themselves.

Othello

Othello is, perhaps, one of Shakespeare's most unusual tragic heroes, a combination of opposites in that he is a 'black' man with a 'perfect soul'. Central to his character then, is what we might call an inversion of the relationship between body and soul. So long as his 'perfect soul' rules his actions, then he is the 'noble Moor', but once he falls victim to his passions, then the relationship between the two is reversed. Information about his character comes to us from a variety of sources in the play; for example he gives information about himself, and others provide details about him, although in all cases we should treat carefully both the sources and the contexts of these remarks. The information which others give about him is of two kinds, positive and negative. We should note that Othello does not appear onstage until the second scene of the play, but even before he does, a sustained attack has already been mounted on his character by Iago and Roderigo. In their view he is proud, self-opinionated, bombastic in his utterance, and a bad judge of others:

> But he, as loving his own pride and purposes,
> Evades them with a bombast circumstance,
> Horribly stuff'd with epithets of war:
>
> (I.1.12–14)

In the opening scene he is variously referred to as 'the Moor' (I.1.40), 'the thicklips' (I.1.66), 'an old black ram' (I.1.88), and finally, 'the devil' (I.1.91). Some critics take the view that Shakespeare may have sought to mobilise the prejudices against 'Moors' that his audience may have shared, at this early point in the play. This is not easy to determine. What we can say, however, is that both Iago and Roderigo, the one having failed to get the lieutenantship that Cassio now holds, and the other having failed to secure Desdemona for himself, are hardly impartial observers. Even when Othello appears, giving us the chance to judge him against this reductive evaluation, the only firm evidence which emerges is that of our eyes (the kind of evidence to which Brabantio, and later he himself, will succumb).

Set against this clearly derogatory view, is that of the Duke of Venice, who holds Othello in high regard, appraising his virtues and entrusting him with the governorship of Cyprus. Desdemona's testimony is also important in that her evaluation of Othello eschews his physical appearance in favour of the qualities of his mind. Montano, the former governor of Cyprus admires him: 'the man commands/Like a full soldier:' (II.1.35–6), and added to that is Cassio's admiring remark after Othello's death that he was 'great of heart' (V.2.362). There is one other, rather curious piece of information which comes from Iago, and which we might therefore expect to be derogatory, but which points ironically towards a strength of character‚ which Othello shares with Cassio, Lodovico, and even Brabantio, and which Iago himself proposes to exploit:

> The Moor a free and open nature too,
> That thinks men honest that but seems to be so:
> And will as tenderly be led by the nose . . .
> As asses are.
>
> (I.3.397–400)

Some critics have, of course, sought to demonstrate that from the outset Iago's opinion of Othello is right, but whatever view we accept, we should follow the example of the Duke of Venice and weigh carefully *all* of the evidence at our disposal.

In addition to what others say of him, Othello tells us a lot about himself. Compared with Iago's earthy and reductive language, his is, indeed, elevated—he almost always speaks in verse—but in the early stages of the play it could hardly be described as 'bombastic'. Rather, his language is open and direct, dignified and yet courteous, revealing a modesty which at times borders almost on self-effacement: 'Rude am I in my speech,/And little blest with the set phrase of peace,' (I.3.81–2). His long description of his courtship of Desdemona, which he says himself will be 'a round unvarnish'd tale' (I.3.90), hardly corroborates the insinuation in Roderigo's earlier claim that he is 'an extravagant and wheeling stranger,/Of here, and everywhere' (I.1.136–7), nor indeed Iago's later description of him as an 'erring barbarian' (I.3.356–7), and as if to underline this, the Duke himself comments on the efficacy of Othello's story (I.3.171). We also learn from Othello that his love for Desdemona represents a principle of 'order', and he gives us no reason to doubt its propriety. Generally, the Othello of the first two acts is a character of impressive dignity and presence, well able to command, and possessing the kind of charisma which diverts our attention from the ambiguous circumstances of his marriage (about which we hear no definitive account). But as he succumbs to the passion of jealousy, based as it is upon suspicion, his rational powers are so perverted that his own view of himself changes. His black face becomes a badge or emblem of his sullied reputation, as Shakespeare now sets out to explore the full dramatic ambiguity of the soul/body paradox which we observed earlier. What in I.3.81–2, seemed to be the product of modesty and courtesy, Othello now views as a deficiency (see III.3.267–70).

His blackness, the deficiencies of his speech, and a debilitating sense of his own age, now replace our earlier positive view of him. During the middle part of the play, after Iago has begun to work on him (III.3) what Othello says about himself should be treated with extreme caution, since we know that he is deluded. Lodovico reminds us (IV.1.260–4) of his former 'noble nature', and 'solid virtue', as a way of keeping before us the Othello of the first two acts of the play, but it is not until after the murder of Desdemona, when the truth begins to emerge, that the pendulum begins to swing back. Horrified though we are at the extravagance of Othello's reactions to Iago's insinuations, (here, if anywhere, the charge of 'bombast' is well-founded) his attempts to justify Desdemona's murder arouse in us a measure of sympathy, partly because we have been privileged to see how it has come about. Though we can hardly excuse Othello's behaviour, we can sympathise with his claim that he is:

An honourable murderer if you will:
For nought did I in hate, but all in honour.
(V.2.295–6)

Though not entirely to blame, he does assume full responsibility for his action as he proceeds to exact from himself the terrible penalty that he now realises he has wrongfully imposed upon Desdemona. His final speech, measured and dignified, recaptures the modesty and directness of his earlier utterances. Moreover, his enactment of a part of his personal history, upon which his claim to nobility rests, contributes to our sense of him as a tragic hero, torn violently between opposed viewpoints, and reconciling them only at the cost of his own life.

Desdemona

Desdemona is altogether more simply drawn. She does embody the principle of 'good' in the play, but Shakespeare takes care to provide her with certain human touches which fill out her character. She is probably younger than Othello, although Brabantio's early references to her as 'O unhappy girl' (I.1.163), and 'a maid, so tender, fair, and happy,' (I.2.66) do not indicate that she is less than adult.

Despite Iago's insinuations, and Othello's later attacks upon her, she remains the most consistent character in the play, although the ambiguous circumstances of her marriage do open her actions to the possibility of misinterpretation. Brabantio initially thinks of her as a victim of Othello's magic charms: 'Damn'd as thou art, thou hast enchanted her,' (I.2.63), and, of course, Iago sees her simply as a passive animal, dominated by a more forceful one: 'an old black ram/Is tupping your white ewe;' (I.1.88–9). But when Desdemona does appear to speak for herself, we are immediately aware of a woman, mature in judgement, perceptive, and in full control of her faculties. She outlines her 'duty' both to her father and to her husband (I.3.180–9), and she is clear and positive about her reasons for having decided to marry Othello. We are impressed too by the faith she inspires in her husband, who responds to Brabantio's churlish allegation that she may be more deceitful than Othello realises, with the comment: 'My life upon her faith:' (I.3.294). We should note in passing that this line, completed with the addition 'honest Iago', also points forward to the fate which awaits both her and Othello, since it will be hers and her husband's faith that Iago will undermine. But at this point in the play we cannot fail to admire the clearness and honesty of Desdemona's character.

As with Othello, there are two viewpoints to consider. The public demonstration of Desdemona's virtues is balanced by a more covert undermining of them as Iago undertakes to instruct Roderigo in what he claims are the habits of Venetian women. (He does the same later to Othello). Desdemona's love is reduced to 'merely a lust of the blood, and a permission of the will.' (I.3.335–6), and therefore cannot last: 'When she is sated with his (Othello's) body, she will find the error of her choice;' (I.3.351–2). Throughout, and particularly in Acts III and IV, Iago emphasises the discrepancy (as he formulates it) between Desdemona's physical beauty, and the corruptness of her soul, and he seeks to persuade Othello that the deceit she practises is somehow typical.

When Iago advances this kind of argument to Desdemona herself, she rejects it as a collection of 'old paradoxes, to make fools laugh i'the alehouse;' (II.138–9), just as she responds later to Emilia's awareness of the sordid ways of the world: 'Beshrew me, if I would do such a wrong,/For the whole world.' (IV.3.77–8). It could be argued that Desdemona's innocence is simply too good to be true, a naïvety which has no place in either Cyprus or Venice. But we must remember that more than any other character in the play, she has a thorough knowledge of 'goodness', although Shakespeare takes pains to make it plausibly human in its appearance. For example, her elopement we have already mentioned, but notice the concern as she waits for Othello's arrival in Cyprus, particularly when she tries to disguise her own anxiousness:

> I am not merry, but I do beguile
> The thing I am, by seeming otherwise.
> (II.1.122–3)

Of course, like her elopement, this comment has a sinister ring to it, and it helps to make Othello's own fall more plausible, but at this point it enables us to engage with the thoughts and feelings of Desdemona as a caring human being, as well as savour the irony of her position. Similarly, later, in a scene of considerable tension and foreboding, we become aware, through her singing of the 'willow' song, of the intensity of her feelings. Here, if anywhere, Desdemona's view of the world could change, since her confidence in human relationships has been shattered, but even after the discussion with Emilia, and her questions about human behaviour, her prayers are finally directed towards eliminating evil, rather than participating in it:

> Good night, good night: God me such usage send
> Not to pick bad from bad, but by bad mend!
> (IV.3.104–5)

There is a sense in which Desdemona is intrinsically incorruptible, although her doubts go some way towards humanising her character. Also, her actions are shown to be extremely vulnerable. Iago illustrates this in his conversation with Cassio just before the lieutenant falls from favour, but the latter continues to assert Desdemona's qualities in the face of a cynical attempt to undermine them. For Cassio she remains 'a most exquisite lady.' (II.3.18), 'a most fresh and delicate creature'

(II.3.20), whose speech is the model of 'perfection' (II.3.25). But to one already corrupted, these claims have no force, and hence she is made to seem naïve in her subsequent pleading for Cassio.

There is, of course, a sense in which all 'good' in the play seems naïve in the face of Iago's cynical and reductive outlook. The point is that Desdemona's openness is made to seem tactless, and in a curious way, childish, in a situation in which it is a quality no longer to be valued. She preserves her integrity for us with her request to Cassio to 'Stay and hear me speak'. (III.3.31), and even her excuse for not being able to produce her handkerchief (III.4.81) cannot except in a reduced context, be considered as deceit. These are all examples of Shakespeare's ability to individualise her character, while at the same time not losing sight of the values she represents within the wider framework of the play. In a number of ways Desdemona is a yardstick by which we can measure the extent of Othello's transformation. From a language they both share in the early part of the play, (Iago says privately: 'O, you are well tun'd now' II.1.199), Othello sinks to a position where Desdemona can no longer understand him: 'I understand a fury in your words/ But not the words.' (IV.2.32–3). Perhaps the final evidence for her consistent devotion comes when, at the point of death, she takes full blame for Othello's action: 'Nobody, I myself, farewell:' (V.2.125).

Iago

Iago is probably the most sophisticated of a long line of Shakespearean villains, and he shares certain characteristics with Richard III in the early tragedy of *Richard III* (1593), Don John, in the comedy *Much Ado About Nothing* (1599), and Claudius in *Hamlet* (1601). Many attempts have been made to account for Iago's evil disposition, and he, himself, adduces a number of motives for his destruction of Othello. The Romantic poet, Samuel Coleridge, concluded that Iago was the embodiment of a 'motiveless malignity for which there need be no explanation, although later critics, such as William Empson in *The Structure of Complex Words*, have sought to vindicate his character from this criticism by drawing attention to his 'realistic' approach to human experience. Whatever the truth of the matter, it seems clear that Shakespeare sought to create more than simply an embodiment of evil, designed merely as a counterbalance to the moral values attributed to Desdemona. Iago's lies are plausible, and there is a grain of truth in his evaluation of experience, but he fools everybody, and his lies are, nonetheless, lies.

Iago is unquestionably evil, but Shakespeare complicates the picture by attributing to him a series of motives for wanting to destroy Othello. But, as with all the other characters in the play, we have to observe carefully the circumstances in which these explanations are advanced, since if we absolve Iago from blame, then we run the risk of devaluing the stature of the tragic hero himself, and of dismissing the entire action as improbable.

The first motive that Iago advances for his disloyalty to Othello concerns his failure to obtain the post of lieutenant which has gone to Cassio. Iago is confident of his own abilities: 'I know my price, I am worth no worse a place.' (I.1.11), but he disparages ruthlessly the abilities and integrity of others. It would appear, then, that Iago is envious of Cassio: 'He has a daily beauty in his life,/That makes me ugly:' (V.1.19–20), but he is equally scathing in his comments upon Othello's judgement, for having preferred the comparatively inexperienced Cassio to himself: 'And I, of whom his eyes had seen the proof,' (I.1.28). Iago hardly ever advances one motive at a time for his actions; Cassio may have a 'daily beauty in his life', but he may also tell Othello of Iago's plans, therefore he must be killed. Similarly, whatever he says to Roderigo, his main objective is to persuade the latter to continue paying him money.

Throughout, Iago's motives revolve around the twin poles of greed and envy. In his soliloquy at the end of Act I, his motive for hating Othello is surprisingly inadequate:

> I hate the Moor,
> And it is thought abroad, that 'twixt my sheets
> He's done my office; I know not if't be true . . .
> Yet I, for mere suspicion in that kind,
> Will do, as if for surety:

> (I.3.384–8)

Later in the play Emilia reminds us of this allegation, and links it with the consistently cynical viewpoint that Iago advances, as she tries to guess who might be responsible for Othello's transformation: 'Some such squire he was,/That turn'd your wit the seamy side without,/And made you suspect me with the Moor.' (IV.2.147–9). It is the same outlook which prompts him to surmise that Cassio is in love with Desdemona: 'That Cassio loves her, I do well believe it;' (II.1.281), and moreover to admit as part of his motive for revenge, his own love for her: 'now I do love her too,/Not out of absolute lust . . . But partly led to diet my revenge,' (II.1.286–9). Evidently, from Emilia's point of view, Iago's cynicism amounts to a disposition of character for which there appears to be no clear reason. Cassio too observes this outspoken frankness in Iago, which he mistakes for 'honesty', and suggests that this is because he is a soldier: 'He speaks home, madam, you may relish him more in the soldier than in the scholar'. (II.1.165–6). And yet we notice that even Cassio is not free from the suspicion of having seduced Iago's wife:

'For I fear Cassio with my night-cap too;' (II.1.302). From these motives we may deduce that Iago's aim is to corrupt. Othello is of 'a constant, noble, loving nature;' (II.1.284), while Desdemona's own 'goodness' will 'make the net/That shall enmesh 'em all.' (II.3.352-3).

There is clearly a sense in which we may regard Iago as an 'individualist', relying as he does upon the power of his 'will' rather than upon any sense of morality. When Roderigo speaks of his 'virtue', he responds contemptuously with: 'Virtue? a fig! 'tis in ourselves, that we are thus,/ or thus: our bodies are gardens, to the which our wills are gardeners,' (I.3.319-20). He rejects outright the notion of 'fate' (a notion which Othello himself uses to account for his own fall: 'Who can control his fate?', V.2.266), and he demonstrates this rejection by controlling for the most part, the plot of the play. He loses no opportunity to lead his victims into making mistakes by preparing the ground carefully with suggestion and interpretation of event, thus depriving them of the power to make independent judgements. Iago's success depends very much upon preserving the secrecy of his designs, and his control of the plot enables him to keep his victims apart for most of the play; when they meet, then they do so only in conditions which he prescribes for them.

Iago occupies the point of view towards which Othello gradually moves. Shakespeare's provision of motives gives his villainy a plausibility which we cannot (in the same way that the characters in the play do not) examine too closely. Iago uses them occasionally as he keeps us dangling in his soliloquies. It is not, therefore, surprising that once his plots are revealed, he refuses to explain them: 'Demand me nothing, what you know, you know,/From this time forth I never will speak word.' (V.2.305-6). Perhaps all that we can really say of Iago is that he exists. In a frightened retort after Othello stabs him he observes maliciously, 'I bleed, sir, but not kill'd' (V.2.289), and even after the hero lies dead, Iago still remains, observing the tragic results of his devilish handiwork.

Roderigo

Although Roderigo is, by comparison, a minor character in the play, he fulfils a vital function in its central action; he illuminates Iago's character and method for us.

Because he is the first to be taken in by Iago's lies, he provides us with an opportunity to glimpse in advance the very means whereby Othello's downfall will be engineered. Although he is a rival for the hand of Desdemona, and continues to pursue her even after she is married, he lacks Othello's presence, yet if the latter can be 'tenderly led by the nose . . ./As asses are.' (I.3.399-400), so also can Roderigo. His lack of awareness of the confidence which Iago places in him makes him something of a comic figure, who commands little of our sympathy. In the opening scene of the play his objections to Iago's past behaviour are easily dismissed, as he rapidly embraces both a derogatory view of Othello, and an inflated sense of the possibilities of his own success in obtaining Desdemona. His language is, perhaps, less coarse than that of Iago, but his viewpoint is identical, as he describes Desdemona's elopement as an act of covert deception:

> Transported with no worse nor better guard,
> But with a knave of common hire, a gondolier,
> To the gross clasps of a lascivious Moor:
> (I.1.124–6)

He convinces Brabantio sufficiently to persuade the old man to change his opinion of him, from one of outright rejection: 'In honest plainness thou hast heard me say/My daughter is not for thee;' (I.1.97–8), to acceptance: 'On, good Roderigo, I'll deserve your pains.' (I.1.184). Roderigo then, becomes a corrupter of others, just as he has become corrupted by Iago. Whenever we encounter him in the play, his wavering resolve is being strengthened by Iago's persuasive rhetoric (which it is designed to expose), as he is cajoled into participating in the plots to discredit first Othello, and then Cassio. His reluctance to take part suggests that he is not totally devoid of moral awareness, but that he is simply too weak to assert himself. He requires considerable prompting, both before and during the course of the first plot to discredit Cassio: 'How now Roderigo,/I pray you, after the lieutenant go.' (II.3.130–1), and before the attempt to murder him he admits:

> I have no great devotion to the deed;
> And yet he has given me satisfying reasons,
> 'Tis but a man gone: forth, my sword, he dies.
> (V.1.8–10)

While we may criticise this reluctance, and perhaps observe the ludicrously comic dismissal of human life here, we should be wary of expecting Roderigo to do more, since the alternative, which Iago invites us to approve, is his own diabolical wilfulness. The pathetic nature of Roderigo's resistance to Iago's suggestions is as nothing compared to the revelations which follow them in the latter's soliloquies. Moreover, Roderigo's final realisation of his own villainy: 'O villain that I am!' (V.1.29) shows an awareness after the event, not unlike that of Othello, except that he never breaks free from Iago who kills him simply in order to maintain the secrecy of his plot.

Brabantio

Brabantio appears only in the first act of the play as both harrassed father and respected Venetian senator. Clearly he knows nothing about Desdemona's elopement, a factor which forces us to question its full propriety, but like Roderigo, he is easily persuaded into believing the worst, even before he has had the opportunity to test the conclusions he is offered. When told of his daughter's elopement in crudely graphic terms, he believes it, using as corroboration a 'dream' that he has had:

> This accident is not unlike my dream,
> Belief of it oppresses me already:
> (I.1.142–3)

We should not be uncritical of this; compare, for example, Banquo's comment in *Macbeth* upon the thoughts which creep into the mind during sleep: 'Restrain in me the cursed thoughts that nature/Gives way to in repose!' (II.1.8–9). Thus, although Brabantio's dream is unquestionably one of foreboding, it gives us as much of a hint about his loss of mental control as it does about the allegedly evil nature of Desdemona's action. Perhaps we should link this to his swift changes of mind in relation to Roderigo. So convinced is he of the nature of his daughter's action that her unexplained absence alone forces him to conclude that it bodes evil: 'It is too true an evil, gone she is,' (I.1.160). We should contrast this easy capitulation with the Duke's careful sifting of evidence at the beginning of Act I Scene 3. When Brabantio confronts Othello, it is with accusations whose origins we recognise as being Iago, and he simply accepts as true (as does Iago), reasons which are in themselves highly speculative: ''Tis probable and palpable to thinking.' (I.2.76).

Brabantio's demise is swift, and an efficient demonstration of the potency of Iago's 'poison':

> And though he in a fertile climate dwell,
> Plague him with flies: though that his joy be joy,
> Yet throw such changes of vexation on't,
> As it may lose some colour.
> (I.1.70–3)

But the victim of this method is sharply at odds with the view of him which emerges from what the Duke of Venice himself says of his qualities. In the Venetian senate he is 'gentle signior,' (I.3.50) and 'Good Brabantio,' (I.3.172) whose counsel and advice are genuinely prized: 'We lack'd your counsel and your help tonight.' (I.3.51). Moreover, the contradictions multiply as Othello himself reveals that Brabantio had actually encouraged his visits, and was as captivated by his stories as Desdemona had been:

> Her father lov'd me, oft invited me,
> Still question'd me the story of my life
> From year to year;
> (I.3.128–30)

The view of another, less hostile Brabantio emerges when the Duke, after having heard and weighed the evidence, says to him: 'Let me speak like yourself, and lay a sentence,/Which as a grise or step may help these lovers/Into your favour.' (I'3'199–200). But the now transformed Brabantio whose feelings of certainty have already fallen victim to Iago's ruthless method, perceives only the equivocal meaning of what the Duke says, and resolves to sustain his discontent in the face of every attempt to appease his condition:

> I never yet did hear
> That the bruis'd heart was pierced through the ear:
> (I.3.219–20)

This failure to respond foreshadows Othello's own refusal to admit the validity of what Desdemona later says in her own defence, and it is ironic that Brabantio's own observation of her deception should later be taken up and used as evidence against her both by Iago and Othello himself. When at the end of the play Gratiano reveals that the marriage of Desdemona to Othello was 'mortal' to Brabantio, (V.2.206), we are tempted to conclude that here is yet another of Iago's victims, whose 'joy' has been perverted into a deadly hate.

Cassio

We have already seen how Othello, Roderigo, and Brabantio are duped by Iago. Cassio is the fourth character to fall victim, but unlike the other three, he is still alive at the end of the play, and takes over the governorship of Cyprus from Othello. Ironically, after having been accused of 'replacing' Othello in Desdemona's affections, he does replace him in another capacity, and one which gives the lie finally to Iago's objections to him. It is Cassio's apparent inexperience that arouses Iago's initial jealousy; he has never, so it is claimed, fought a battle, and 'mere prattle without practice/is all his soldiership:' (I.1.26–7). The denigration of Cassio is as extreme as that of Othello himself. When the young lieutenant first appears, it is as an emissary of the Venetian senate, but we notice immediately that he and Iago do not have the same outlook at all. The latter's cynical account of Othello's marriage is met with incomprehension from Cassio:

IAGO: Faith, he tonight hath boarded a land carrack:
If it prove lawful prize, he's made for ever.
CASSIO: I do not understand.
IAGO: He's married.

(I.1.50–2)

This is the first of a number of occasions on which Cassio refuses to accept Iago's crude analysis of events (see also II.3.15–25), and we notice that throughout he is generous in his dealings with others. Cassio, nonetheless, is vulnerable, and paradoxically because of his strengths as much as of his weaknesses. Iago claims from the outset that he is 'A fellow almost damn'd in a fair wife,' (I.1.21) whose physical attractiveness is 'To be suspected, fram'd to make women false:' (I.3.396). Cassio is courteous, but the gestures with which he welcomes both Desdemona and Emilia to Cyprus will be construed as lecherous advances by Iago: 'Ay, smile upon her, do: I will catch you in your own courtesies:' (II.1.169–70), and will provide the 'ocular proof' of Desdemona's infidelity. The only courtesy that Cassio eschews (and we should not take this as too serious a sign of weakness), is that of drinking to excess: 'I am unfortunate in the infirmity and dare not task my weakness with any more.' (II.3.37–8). He is persuaded, Roderigo provokes him into a quarrel, and he loses his 'reputation' as well as risks the peace of the island. His demise is, of course, necessary to the plot of the play since Cassio's innocent importuning of Desdemona will ironically provide the grounds upon which suspicion of their collusion in deceit is to be founded. In addition, Cassio's drunken lack of co-ordination, though comic in its immediate effect, foreshadows Othello's more serious loss of control as he begins to fear the safety of his own 'reputation'.

But, as in the case of a number of other characters in the play, Cassio is more than simply a cardboard figure. Setting aside for a moment the question of 'time' in the play, it is puzzling that Cassio, a 'proper man' in so many respects, should consort with a character like Bianca, whom a number of the other characters think is a prostitute. If we look closely at when she first appears we find that Cassio greets her with 'my most fair Bianca?', and 'sweet love' (III.4.168–9). Moreover, we notice that the only circumstances in which they appear together on stage are those which Iago has either contrived, or can take advantage of for the purpose of his plotting. But if that is said, their relationship seems altogether more down-to-earth than that of Desdemona and Othello, hinting, but giving no real substance to the view that Cassio is a 'ladies' man'. The ambiguity of Cassio's relationship with Bianca seems therefore, deliberate. Furthermore, when we observe Bianca's pangs of jealousy at Cassio's production of Desdemona's handkerchief, his response seems to contradict flatly the view that she is a character of no consequence:

Throw your vile guesses in the devil's teeth,
From whence you have them; you are jealous now
That this is from some mistress, some remembrance.
No, by my faith Bianca.

(III.4.182–5)

If we fail to respond positively to pleas of this kind, then we run the risk of branding Cassio as a liar, which he clearly is not. On the other hand, even he himself admits to Iago that his affections are not seriously engaged: 'I marry her? what? a customer;' (IV.1.119). While there seems to be little doubt of Bianca's affection for him, Shakespeare seems also to want to indicate that Cassio is both a man of honour, and an experienced participant in more obviously worldly things. Though nothing more is heard of Bianca after the beginning of Act V, Cassio's relationship with her does not prevent him from becoming the ruler of Cyprus. When the details of Iago's plots finally emerge Cassio openly states 'Dear general, I did never give you cause.' (V.2.300), and we should weigh this defence carefully against any suggestion that he behaves improperly in relation either to Desdemona, or to Bianca.

Emilia

For much of the play, Emilia's role is a subsidiary one. Though she is the wife of Iago, she is ignorant of the real nature of his plots, and she even aids his designs without any awareness of their consequences. For example, she is asked to persuade Desdemona to plead for Cassio's reinstatement, and she gives Iago the handkerchief which will play so large a part in convincing Othello of his wife's guilt. Shakespeare portrays Emilia in a 'realistic' light, attributing to her (as with Cassio) strengths and weaknesses, combining in her character qualities of loyalty and service, with a commitment also to the more worldly side of human nature. Iago dismisses her as a typical woman, chiding, licentious, and deceitful, but she responds firmly to his criticism with a statement which echoes throughout the remainder of the play: 'You ha' little cause to say so.' (II.1.108). Emilia tolerates her husband's cynicism and recognises it for what it is, but she does not suspect Iago of outright evil. Also, she observes and comments upon the generalised patterns of human behaviour against which the relationship of Othello and Desdemona might, as it changes, be measured:

'Tis not a year or two shows us a man:
They are all but stomachs, and we all but food;
They eat us hungerly, and when they are full
They belch us.

(III.4.100–3)

She is obviously more realistic in her appraisal of human nature than
Desdemona in that she sees both its positive and negative aspects, and
her approach to life in general is a pragmatic one. Even so, and despite
the fact that she can offer an insincere argument for overthrowing
moral standards (see IV.3.70–103), she is in no doubt about the distinctions between good and evil, and can recognise them. Perhaps
Bianca's response to the accusation of 'strumpet' that Emilia levels
against her, provides us with as concise an evaluation of Emilia's
character as we could wish for:

> I am no strumpet, but of life as honest
> As you that thus abuse me.   (V.1.121–2)

Emilia is, therefore, particularly qualified to analyse the moral nature
of Othello's murder of Desdemona. Moreover, she represents a crucial
link in the chain whereby Iago's villainy will be finally exposed. It is
Emilia who makes public the fact of Desdemona's death in a way which
breaks Iago's hold on the action. It is ironical, nonetheless, that she has
to relinquish the loyalty which Iago has hitherto traded upon: ''Tis
proper I obey him, but not now:' (V.2.197), but her continued insistence
that she should be allowed to speak makes her instrumental in restoring
to language a new propriety. Moreover, the revelation of Iago's villainy,
which surprises her, places her in an almost identical position to Desdemona as the forsaken mistress, and she reinforces the comparison with
her recalling of the 'willow' song after Iago has stabbed her. Desdemona's 'A guiltless death I die.' (V.2.123) is balanced by the equally
truthful nature of Emilia's dying statement, which re-unites the acts of
'speaking' and 'thinking' which Iago has striven to separate throughout:

> So come my soul to bliss, as I speak true;
> So speaking as I think, I die, I die.   (V.2.251–2)

The language of 'Othello'

The Elizabethan stage contained no scenery, and so the burden of ex-
pounding the action rested firmly upon the dramatist's and actor's
combined powers to evoke a sense of place, and atmosphere, through
language. *Othello* employs these resources to the full, both in terms of
the play's theme (as Emilia's final comment illustrates), and at a more
fundamental technical level. Critics have always been aware of the
'poetry' of *Othello*, of the intensity and pressure of its figurative language, but this should not blind us to the wide variety of expression that
the play employs, ranging from the formal and magnificent utterances
of the hero himself, to a more flexible and natural language, not far
removed from that of everyday speech. We should however, guard

against falling into the trap of thinking that Shakespeare's purpose was to imitate the language of everyday life, or indeed, that Elizabethans spoke in blank verse. The variations in style fulfil a dramatic purpose, and we should see them as part of the wider formal structure of the play.

The basic metre which Shakespeare uses is the iambic pentameter, a combination of five strong, and five weakly stressed syllables distributed alternately throughout a single line. But as Shakespeare's own style developed, so the metrical patterns of his blank verse became more flexible, as he sought to reflect more complex states of mind in his characters. In a play like *Othello*, in which formal order is attacked and destroyed, we might reasonably expect to find some attempt to reflect this in the structure of the play's language. How this works can be discovered in the opening scene of the play, in Brabantio's speech after he has realised that Desdemona is missing. Brabantio begins with a positive, measured conclusion, and the ominous evenness of its tone is dogmatic in its certainty and seemingly firm in its grasp of the thought of what the future holds:

> ∪ / ∪ / ∪ / ∪ / ∪ /
> It is too true an evil, gone she is,
> ∪ / ∪ / ∪ / ∪ / ∪ /
> And what's to come of my despised time
> ∪ / ∪ / ∪ /
> Is nought but bitterness. (I.1.160–2)

These lines, however, contain an additional tension in that we already know that his 'truth' is fabricated and cannot therefore be established so simply or so certainly. But we also observe that what begins as formal blank verse disintegrates rapidly into fragmented prose as Brabantio's language begins to register his own mental confusion. The breakdown begins with his 'Now Roderigo,' (I.1.162), correcting itself momentarily in the following line although the parenthesis reinforces the sense of a mind gradually losing control:

> ∪ / ∪ / ∪ / ∪ / ∪ /
> Where didst thou see her? (O unhappy girl!) (I.1.163)

It culminates in an extremely awkward verse bordering on prose in its variegated rhythms:

> How didst thou know 'twas she? (O thou deceivest me
> Past thought!) What said she to you? Get more tapers,
> Raise all my kindred, are they married, think you? (I.1.165–7)

Brabantio's language conveys here the sense of a mind wrestling to exert control over itself, but failing to do so, as rhythm and metre begin to collide with each other.

Throughout the play we observe a tension between the formal order of public expression, varied though its rhythms often are, and the prospect of mental chaos which lies just beneath the surface of the language. What happens in Brabantio's speech operates on a much larger scale in Othello's language as the 'harmony' of his utterance is 'untuned'. Brabantio's speech descends to prose, the idiom of Iago, just as the rhythm and order of Othello's language is destroyed when he contemplates the adultery of Desdemona and Cassio:

Lie with her, lie on her?—We say lie on her, when
they belie her,—lie with her, zounds, that's fulsome!
Handkerchief—confessions—handkerchief! To confess . . .

Pish! Noses, ears and lips. Is't possible? Confess?
—Handkerchief?—O devil!   (*He falls down*)   (IV.1.35-43)

The mental turmoil here is a far cry from the ordered speech of Othello's defence of his marriage (I.3.76-94), or indeed from the nervous hold on formal expression that he manages to re-assert in his final speech in the play (V.2.339-57).

More difficult in *Othello*, however, are those occasions where despite its formality, there appears to be some sort of gulf between utterance and meaning. Often the Duke's 'sentences' (I.3.199-209), which comprise-a series of rhymed couplets in iambic pentameter form, are considered so formal as to reflect some uneasiness on his part at the domestic problem he has had to solve. Here the question of 'tone' is important, and those who are critical of Othello's action and character at this point in the play will, doubtless, interpret the Duke's speech in this way. But the context of his remarks (which Brabantio himself perverts in his equally formal reply), suggests that he is imparting a form of wisdom which he feels that a more temperate Brabantio might have done just as well. An equally difficult example occurs later in the play when Othello, after having been convinced by Iago's lies, swears to exact vengeance upon Desdemona. Here the formal delivery of the lines is used to emphasise the nature of Othello's mistake as we see him squandering his dignity in a series of empty gestures. Because we are aware of the mistake he is making, we are in a position to appreciate the parody of order which the rhythm of these lines reflect:

Now do I see 'tis true; look here Iago,
All my fond love thus do I blow to heaven, . . .
'Tis gone.
Arise, black vengeance from thy hollow cell,   (III.3.451-4)

This is a very different Othello from the 'noble' hero of the first two acts of the play.

The gesture which Othello makes in this speech raises the much more complex question of precisely how language and gesture are deployed throughout the play. We have already observed the conflict between 'appearance' and 'reality', and the paradoxes to which it leads. We must now observe carefully what each character understands from the words and gestures of another. For example, Iago's 'stops' which Othello mistakes for indications of his reluctance to utter an unpalatable truth, are really being used as ways of supporting his villainous argument. Othello recognises the devices, and their potential evil, but he does not associate them with 'honest' Iago:

> For such things in a false disloyal knave
> Are tricks of custom; but in a man that's just,
> They are close denotements, working from the heart,
> That passion cannot rule.
>
> (III.3.125-8)

Similarly in a scene which Iago engineers to give Othello 'occular proof' of Desdemona's guilt, the victim 'must conster/Poor Cassio's smiles, gestures, and light behaviour,/Quite in the wrong.' (IV.1.101-3). We might contrast Iago's gestures with those of Othello who is unaware of what they signify, and whose own 'stops', as we have seen, reflect a genuine mental turmoil. Also, again by way of contrast to Iago, we might notice Emilia's questioning repetitions of the word 'husband' in V.2.141-55, which convey a genuine sense of shock at the truth which is only now beginning to emerge. Iago's 'echoing' of Othello's words earlier (III.3.105ff.) are, we know, for a very different purpose. We shall find many examples in the play of the way in which Shakespeare seeks to convey different levels of emotional response in his characters to the situations in which they find themselves. The result is a drama of considerable linguistic subtlety.

Imagery

Let us now turn to one particular aspect of the language of *Othello*, its imagery. Here we should distinguish between two uses of imagery, the one designed to communicate a vivid and immediate effect, and the other which seeks to weave a 'pattern', helping to draw together the various strands of the dramatic action into some coherent design. This principle of design is especially necessary when we remember that in performance the spectator has no control of the pace at which a play moves forward, unlike the reader of, say, a novel, who has absolute control over the pace of his reading. The dramatist therefore, has to find ways of helping his audience to recall what has already taken place, and to arouse certain expectations of what is to come. The interplay between these elements is usually the source of dramatic irony. The general term that we use for this design is 'structure', and it is part of the task of the literary critic to try to recognise and establish plausible relationships of meaning between the various elements which make up the play's structure. The use and distribution of particular images throughout a play like *Othello*, is an important aspect of its structure.

One of the functions of imagery in a Shakespeare play is to help us to visualise more clearly particular facets of dramatic action and character. For example, Othello's control of military affairs is vividly protrayed in an image which suggests extraordinary powers of endurance.

> The tyrant custom, most grave senators,
> Hath made the flinty and steel couch of war
> My thrice-driven bed of down: (I.3.229–31)

That a 'flinty and steel couch of war' should become a 'thrice-driven bed of down', captures in vivid visual terms Othello's capacity to exert control over adverse conditions. Lodovico uses a slightly different image to convey the same idea when he later refers to Othello's 'solid virtue' which: 'The shot of accident, nor dart of chance,/Could neither graze nor pierce.' (IV.1.262–4). But in addition to presenting us with vivid visual pictures, images are often designed to communicate *feeling*, and to elicit some sort of non-visual response from us. The two examples quoted indicate that we should not only visualise these descriptions of Othello, but we must also *evaluate* his qualities as a character capable of exerting such control. Thus our sympathies are either engaged, as they are in the first example, or alienated, as they are in the second.

However, the play contains more complex images which reflect, in concentrated form, a major part of the tragic action. One such occurs at the point when Othello confronts Desdemona after having shocked Lodovico with his intemperate behaviour towards her. Othello's loss of control is extreme, and extends even to his failure to understand the true meaning of what his wife says. When she asks 'Alas, what ignorant sin have I committed?' (IV.2.72), he seizes on the equivocal meaning of the word 'committed' (in a manner similar to that of Brabantio's response to the Duke's 'sentences' in I.3.216–7):

> What, committed?
> Committed! O thou public commoner!
> I should make very forges of my cheeks,
> That would to cinders burn up modesty,
> Did I but speak thy deeds. (IV.2.74–8)

On the visual level Othello is depicting the intensity of his blushes were he to speak of the indecent actions that he believes Desdemona has committed. But the word 'forges' is made to carry a considerable and rich burden of ambiguity here. The blushes would convert Othello's cheeks into 'forges' (the blacksmith's fires), but this would have the effect of falsifying (forging) the naturally black colour of his face, just as he believes Desdemona's 'fair' appearance is now a 'forgery'. 'Modesty' is converted into the fuel which feeds this imaginary fire, and Othello's red cheeks reflect his own embarrassment as he receives the heat from the fire of Desdemona's imagined lust. We might also note here that the 'blacksmith' image hints at Othello's kinship with Vulcan, the smithy of the Gods who was cuckolded by Venus and Mars. Thus, in addition to our having a vivid sense of what Othello thinks of the deception he believes Desdemona has been practising, we also respond to the tragic irony of his position.

These are just a few of the many examples of the different uses to which Shakespeare puts poetic language in *Othello*. But they do form part of a pattern of recurring images, whose function is to keep before us the issues and conflicts which comprise the action of the play. Iago's cynical interpretation of experience derives its power from his consistent ability to visualise human beings *reduced*, often to the level of animals. His description of Othello as 'an old black ram', and of Desdemona as a 'white ewe' (I.1.88-9) are obvious examples, and we might add to this the view of the marriage as 'a frail vow betwixt an erring barbarian and a super-subtle Venetian' (I.3.356-7). But this is part of the image of humanity that Othello himself moves towards as he falls victim to Iago's potent 'medicine' of deception. Thus, when Desdemona weeps in the presence of Lodovico, Othello interprets her gesture in the following manner:

> O devil, devil!
> · If that the earth could teem with women's tears
> Each drop she falls would prove a crocodile:
> (IV.1.239-41)

A little later in the same scene, having been told that Cassio is to replace him as governor of Cyprus, he storms off with the exclamation: 'Goats and monkeys!' (IV.1.259). Significantly, in his final speech of the play, it is the 'animal' in himself that Othello kills: 'I took by the throat the circumcised dog,/And smote him thus.' (V.2.336-7).

As a contrast to this reductive view of humanity, we should notice the ways in which Desdemona is described. Cassio refers to her as 'The divine Desdemona' (II.1.73), and Othello early in the play calls her a 'fair warrior' and his 'soul's joy' (II.1.182-4). Even Roderigo, naïve in the face of Iago's cynical outlook characterises her as being 'full of most blest condition' (II.1.247). Images of divinity, perfection, and order, are used to describe her, the most prophetic of which is Othello's comment immediately before his own fall into chaos:

Excellent wretch, perdition catch my soul
But I do love thee, and when I love thee not,
Chaos is come again.
(III.3.91-3)

Finally, having realised the magnitude of his error, Othello revalues Desdemona, likening her to a precious jewel which he has cast away: 'of one whose hand,/Like the base Indian, threw a pearl away,/Richer than all his tribe:' (V.2.347-9). These two contrasting sets of images provide a foundation for some of the more intricate features of the dramatic action, and contribute to the overall structure of the play.

Dramatic irony

Shakespeare's use of dramatic irony in *Othello* is extensive, involving both situations and characters. Irony arises from our awareness of the discrepancy between what the characters themselves believe is happening, and what is actually taking place. For example, because Iago tells us what he intends to do with his victims, we can judge the disparity between the knowledge he provides for us, and their comparative ignorance of his designs. Roderigo, Brabantio, Cassio, and finally, Othello are all ignorant of some aspects of the situations into which Iago forces them, and this culminates in the supreme tragic irony when Othello believes that in killing Desdemona he is acting in accordance with the dictates of Justice. Indeed, at the very point in Act V, Scene 2 where he considers in soliloquy the irrevocable nature of his action, he claims that her very 'breath' has the power to pervert the course of Justice; it can 'almost persuade/Justice herself to break her sword:' (V.2.15-16). Although *he* believes that the murder he is about to commit is lawful, we know that Desdemona's 'breath' has neither the power nor the inclination to pervert Justice in this way. In fact, the opposite is true; had Othello responded to Desdemona's qualities more positively here, then he would have acted in a fair and just manner. As it is, he misreads the sign of her purity, and decides to kill her. Here we are in a position to appreciate in the fullest sense, the way in which the 'appearance' as defined by Othello, is made to contrast with what we know to be the 'reality'. But the situation is more complicated, even, than that. There is a double irony involved in that Othello comes to believe that there is a discrepancy between Desdemona's 'appearance' and what he alleges she really is, and that this is, in fact, a feature of human experience in a more general sense; for example, just as he is persuaded to believe in the inevitability of his own fate:

> Yet 'tis the plague of great ones,
> Prerogativ'd are they less than the base,
> 'Tis destiny, unshunnable, like death:
> Even then this forked plague is fated to us
> When we do quicken:
>   (III.3.277–81)

so he also accepts the dubious wisdom of Iago's later pronouncement, that Desdemona's apparent deception is, in fact, a hellish joke at man's expense:

> O, 'tis the spite of hell, the fiend's arch-mock,
> To lip a wanton in a secure couch,
> And to suppose her chaste.   (IV.1.70–2)

These two statements, placed in the mouths of deceiver and victim contribute to the pattern of irony which emerges in the play. Indeed, while Othello is led to believe that his own disgrace accords with the very workings of fate itself, we look beyond the local context of his remark, to the more general Christian notion of the 'fall of man', and of the traditional conflict between 'good' and 'evil'.

In addition to what is generally called situational irony of this kind, there is also verbal irony, more localised in its effect. For example, Iago's grim comments about Othello's 'openness' or Cassio's handsomeness (I.3.395ff.) are, in effect, satiric indications of what in certain circumstances may be construed as weaknesses. Iago's ironic detachment from his victims is a stance which he invites us to share, but the play never allows us to come too close to the position he occupies. Perhaps one of the best examples of this kind of irony occurs when, for the first time in the play, Othello is forced to question the validity of the very 'parts' which earlier, in Act I Scene 2 he was convinced would show his character to full advantage (I.2.31–3). It is characteristic of Shakespeare's treatment of his hero here, that he does not allow him a soliloquy until he has been brought to the point of doubting his own adequacy:

> Haply for I am black,
> And have not those soft parts of conversation
> That chamberers have, or for I am declin'd
> Into the vale of years—yet that's not much—
>   (III.3.267–70)

His 'blackness', now no longer a neutral 'fact', assumes a new significance, while his earlier skill in 'conversation' is now thought to be inadequate. Othello's 'blackness' will, ultimately become the symbol of evil itself, while his loss of 'conversation' (in a literal as well as a metaphorical sense) will indicate the extent to which the harmonious language, which he shared with Desdemona in the first two acts of the play, has been destroyed. Thus, at this crucial point in the action, Othello's conception of himself does not accord with our knowledge of his character and his predicament. His description of his deficiencies seems ironical to us, because we know more than he does about his situation. Throughout the play there are many examples of irony, deepening our awareness of the nature of the tragic action, and controlling our responses to character and situation.

Scenes and structure

Our concern with imagery has really been a concern with some of the fundamental details of dramatic structure. Another basic unit of structure is the 'scene', since it is through the careful positioning of individual scenes in the play that a pattern of meaning begins to emerge. Scenes are usually separated from each other by distinct pauses as one group of characters leaves the stage and is replaced by another. An obvious example occurs at the end of Act I Scene 1 when the stage is cleared, so that Act I Scene 2 can begin at Othello's lodgings. The pause signifies a change of place, but it also creates a tension since we now eagerly await the confrontation between Brabantio and Othello that Iago and Roderigo have engineered. In this connection the entry of Cassio at I.2.34, increases the tension even further. But we notice also in the play that certain changes of focus (not place) occur within individual scenes, rather similar to the way in which a film camera focuses now on one object, then on another. Although these are not 'scenes' in the strict sense of the term, they are comparable units of design through which the action gradually unfolds. For example, in Act I Scene 1 the street dialogue between Iago and Roderigo acts as a kind of prologue, and is followed by another dialogue, this time involving Brabantio. But the prologue, which ends with Roderigo's comment: 'Here is her father's house, I'll call aloud.' (I.1.74), has already provided us with information which gives the second dialogue an ironical twist as we see the old man being manipulated. In this way we accumulate knowledge of the various stages of the action. We may notice much later on in the play, at III.4 the appearance of the Clown in a dialogue which acts as a prologue to the interview between Othello and Desdemona, and which focuses specifically on the different meanings of particular words. The linguistic uncertainty which the Clown promotes, foreshadows the wider uncertainty which Othello feels as he tries to extract offensive meanings from the words that Desdemona uses:

OTHELLO: Give me your hand; this hand is moist, my lady.

DESDEMONA: It yet hath felt no age, nor known no sorrow.
OTHELLO: This argues fruitfulness, and liberal heart;
             Hot, hot and moist, this hand of yours requires
             A sequester from liberty;

                                                    (III.4.32-6)

Just as for the Clown the word 'lie' admits of alternative meanings, so
here the words 'hot' and 'moist' suggest for Othello sexual licence,
whereas for Desdemona they signify innocence and youth. This kind of
juxtaposition serves to enlarge the scope of the play's concern.

The ordering of incidents is even more revealing in Act I Scene 3,
which comprises *four* separate movements: (1) the dialogue concerning
the activities of the Turkish fleet (2) the 'trial' of Othello (3) The dialogue between Iago and Roderigo (which echoes the opening dialogue
of the play) (4) Iago's concluding soliloquy. Clearly, Shakespeare seeks
to build a pattern here which will help us to compare the values which
inform the attitudes and actions of the characters involved. Using his
powers of right judgement, the Duke weighs the evidence in a matter of
political importance. We then observe the application of that judgement to a more critical domestic issue, thus establishing a connection
between the 'domestic' and 'political' worlds of the play. Moreover,
because of the lack of information we are exposed to the competing
claims of both the negative and positive arguments surrounding
Othello's marriage, and we are encouraged to judge its propriety for
ourselves. Thus we become *involved* in the very dilemma in which
Othello himself will later be placed. Dramatically, the positioning of
Iago's soliloquy at the end rather than the beginning of Act I is crucial.
His discussion with Roderigo reinforces in our minds an already linger-
ing doubt, but it is at the point when our resolve is at its weakest that
Iago steps forward to draw us into his confidence. We are tempted here,
as elsewhere in the play, to approve his frankness, although we must
remember that his motive is entirely evil. By noticing how skilfully
Shakespeare has positioned these 'scenes' and episodes, we gain a
deeper understanding of how the play works.

These scenes are, of course, related to each other in a chronological
sequence. But there are a number of examples in the play of repetitions
of incident separated from each other by larger spaces in the action.
Notice for example, that the events of Act I Scene 3 are repeated as
Othello, like the Duke of Venice, is forced to make two related judgements, the first the political one involving Cassio and the safety of the
island (II.3.195ff.), and the second a domestic one involving Desdemona
(III.3.451ff.). But although the situation Othello is placed in resembles
that of the Duke, his behaviour accords more with that of Brabantio.

These are only a few of the many examples in the play of the positioning of scenes and incidents which serve to enrich the dramatic action. In each case we should observe carefully the characters involved, and also the context in which these incidents take place. It is this complex web of incident and character which makes the play's structure so complex and dramatically effective.

The time-scale of 'Othello'

Shakespeare's treatment of time in *Othello* raises a problem. For over a century critics have been aware of the discrepancies in the play's time-scale, and have suggested that the inconsistencies are the result of Shakespeare's own uncompleted revisions of his manuscript. In *Shakespearean Tragedy*, A.C. Bradley distinguished between 'Short Time' and 'Long Time', explaining their functions in the following way:

> It is not the case that 'Short Time' is wanted only to produce an impression of vehemence and haste, and 'Long Time' for probability. The 'Short Time' is equally wanted for probability: for it is grossly improbable that Iago's intrigue should not break down if Othello spends a week or weeks between the successful temptation and his execution of justice. . . .
>
> The place where 'Long Time' is required is not *within* Iago's intrigue. 'Long Time' is required simply and solely because the intrigue and its circumstances presuppose a marriage consummated and an adultery possible, for (let us say) some weeks. (p.363)

This is a difficult explanation, but Bradley's point seems a fair one, and rather supports the view that there is considerable variation in the pace of the action. We are aware, for example, that the entire action of Act I takes place within the space of one night. Similarly, it would appear that because of the haste of Othello's mission to Cyprus, he and Desdemona have not had the opportunity to consummate their marriage. It would appear also that Othello's arrival in Cyprus, the demise of Cassio, and Iago's temptings take place on the afternoon, night, and morning following each other. The speed of events here gives some substance to Bradley's view that the 'Short Time' scheme lends credibility to Iago's plotting, although it does not entirely account for the speed of Othello's own fall. But we are a little startled to find that in Act III Scene 4, immediately following Othello's temptation and fall, Bianca chides Cassio for not having visited her for a week:

> What, keep a week away? seven days and nights?
> Eight score eight hours, and lovers' absent hours,
> More tedious than the dial, eight score times?
> (III.4.170–3)

Our impression is that no such interval of time has elapsed between Act III Scene 3, and Act III Scene 4. Similarly, and without any impression of the slackening of the momentum of the plot, in Act IV Scene 1 Othello overhears part of Cassio's account of his meeting with Bianca: 'I was t'other day talking on the sea-bank, with certain Venetians . . .' (IV.1.132). Here again, the details conflict with our sense of the forward pressure of the plot. It may well be, however, that the purpose of these details is to convey an *impression*, rather than to convince us of their literal truth, and that while in the study they present us with problems of a logical nature, in the theatre they contribute more immediately to the atmosphere of the play. As an example, let us take Lodovico's appearance, also in Act IV Scene 1. It serves to recall the former 'noble' Othello, but it also suggests that some time has elapsed since he is now to be recalled to Venice: 'For as I think, they do command him home,/ Deputing Cassio in his government.' (IV.1.231-2). It is hardly likely that just having been sent to Cyprus, Othello would be immediately recalled, so that it would appear that a detail of this kind is introduced to further the play's thematic design, and to suggest a series of comparisons and contrasts, rather than to support some kind of uniform time-scale. Whatever the explanations, it is clear that while Iago's plot requires speed, it cannot move too fast since it would cease to be believable, and would affect seriously our own valuation of Othello's character. It may well be that Shakespeare chose to emphasise the intensity of the drama, but sought to reinforce its plausibility by including also a 'background' against which this intensity could be measured.

Part 4

Hints for study

WHEN READING A PLAY we should always guard against the temptation to treat it as though it were a novel. This is often a difficult point to grasp, but we must always bear in mind that a play is designed primarily to be performed, usually in a particular type of building, a theatre, rather than to be read privately. The novelist's medium is solely the words on the page, and what they contain in the way of meaning gives us the information we require to imagine fully characters and situations. The novelist is also in complete control of the *pace* with which his story unfolds, just as the reader, for his part, is able to control the speed at which he reads it.

But in a play, the kind of detailed description of the lives, relationships, and situations of particular characters that we expect from a novel, is absent, partly because the sheer pressure of performance in a particular place at a particular time makes their inclusion impossible. Also, because his words are designed to be spoken by actors, the dramatist cannot halt the flow of his play, just as members of the theatre audience cannot ask that the action be stopped for a moment to allow individuals to ponder particular details. In a play the dramatist can only work *through* the mouths of his characters, unlike the novelist who can adopt a series of different narrative postures. The action of a play is *embodied* in the characters who present it.

With this in mind we should always remember that in a dialogue in a play our attention is not engaged solely by what the speaker is saying, but also by the actions and responses of the character who is listening. On the printed page a dramatic dialogue seems somehow incomplete. Only in performance does it achieve fullness. Here the physical characteristics of speaker and listener, tones of voice, movements, gestures, and facial expressions all contribute to the play's meaning. Consider, for example, Othello's *silence* at the opening of Act I Scene 2. Iago and Roderigo have, in the previous scene already claimed that his speech is bombastic and his attitude self-centred. But during the first seventeen lines of Act I Scene 2 he speaks only one half-line, and that in the most enigmatic manner imaginable: ' 'Tis better as it is.' (I.2.6). In order to appreciate the full dramatic impact of this silence, we are required not only to recall what has gone before, but also to *visualise* this confrontation between a garrulous but deceitful villain and a distinctly unyielding hero whose own appearance and utterance are ambiguous. When we read this scene, we are required to *infer* information about the visual aspects of this dialogue, the tones of voice in which both characters speak, their physical gestures, their appearance, and so on. And of course, as we have seen in the case of *Othello* particularly, this practical necessity of visualising the stage action is used by Shakespeare as an important principle of dramatic design. Throughout we are asked to observe the discrepancies between what we *see* and what we *hear*. Moreover, our understanding of what the Elizabethan theatre looked like, and our sense of the conventions that it imposed upon dramatist, actors, and audience alike, contributes even further to the substance and meaning of the play. All this is part of the adjustment of imaginative perception that we need to make in order to understand fully the text of a play. We must always remember that what we read in the study is really a blueprint for performance, and not a substitute for it.

Characters

In a Shakespeare play characters appear on the stage fully formed, as it were, and any information about their backgrounds or their past lives is only admissable insofar as it is *strictly relevant* to the dramatic action itself. We should be on our guard against questions like 'What kind of personality does Iago have?' since this assumes that he possesses traits of character in addition to those which Shakespeare chose to use in his play. If we think of 'character' in this context as an agency through which the action of the play is revealed to the audience, then we shall avoid the dangers of this kind of question.

How therefore, can we equate this view of dramatic characterisation with the notion that Shakespeare 'humanises' the characters in his plays by giving them traits which make them seem more than simply puppets? We have already seen how he does this in *Othello* with characters like Desdemona, Bianca, Cassio, and Emilia; we know what these characters stand for in the play, but their actions and attitudes are also given some limited plausibility within the confines of the dramatic action. But equally, we cannot enquire too closely into the deeper motivations of a character like Iago. Although he, himself suggests to us a number of motives for his villainy, they do not really stand up to close scrutiny, and we are forced to think of him more obviously in terms of the *function* he fulfils within the overall design of the play.

Bearing this in mind, we should take great care with questions like: 'Why doesn't Othello ask Desdemona straight away in Act III Scene 3 if she has committed adultery with Cassio?'. This is not so simple a question as it seems, nor can we answer it satisfactorily by saying that there is some psychological deficiency in Othello's own character which was there from the start and which refuses to allow him to take this obvious and positive step. Nor is it simply a question of saying that this is how Shakespeare stretches his material out for a further two acts. If we say that Othello's refusal to confront Desdemona directly is a 'flaw' in his character, then we are faced with the difficulty of justifying his status as tragic hero in the play. So obvious a flaw, indicating a radical personal failure to perceive the truth would force us to relinquish both our sympathy and admiration for him. If this is what Shakespeare intended, then why does he take pains to show how many other characters in the play are deceived by appearances? The affairs involving Roderigo, Brabantio, Cassio, Emilia, and even Lodovico would, in such a context prove to be largely redundant, or at best indications of badly conceived plotting on Shakespeare's part. The fact that Othello shares this failure of perception with a host of other characters in the play suggests that the assumptions he holds about human behaviour before Act III Scene 3 are of a general nature, not peculiar to himself alone, and that even after this point in the play, he is convinced that his new viewpoint is a generally held one. It is no accident that Iago always speaks in generalities, as he seeks to persuade all those with whom he comes into contact, that his opinion is one which is generally held by all:

I know our country disposition well;
In Venice they do not let God see the pranks
They dare not show their husbands: their best conscience
Is not to leave undone, but keep unknown.
(III.3.205–9)

By the end of Act IV Scene 1, Iago can allow his victim to speak for him: 'And his own courses will denote him so,/That I may save my speech:' (IV.1.275–6). Of course Iago seeks to replace one set of generally held assumptions with another which violates its integrity. That violation finds an ironical echo in Othello's own appearance, which represents a concrete embodiment of the dramatic conflict between 'appearance' and 'reality' which we observed earlier. Thus, the gradual emergence of these shifts in the values which Othello holds, tell us very little about his 'character' or his 'personality', but a lot about the ways in which Shakespeare seeks to dramatise a moral conflict of a very elemental kind. Or, to put it perhaps a little crudely, the character of Othello represents a kind of dramatic cipher, not a person, and when we are dealing with questions about character and motive in Shakespeare's plays we must always bear this in mind.

Essay questions and revision

Here are some questions which focus on particular aspects of *Othello*:

(1) Comment on the view that the reasons for Othello's downfall lie in his own character.

(2) Discuss the ways in which Othello gradually becomes aware of his own deficiencies in the play.

(3) What do you consider to be the significance of Othello's death at the end of the play? Does it achieve anything?

(4) What is the significance of the episodes involving Cassio and Bianca in *Othello*.

(5) Is Desdemona's character too good to be true? Show from your use of particular examples, how Shakespeare draws her character in *Othello*.

(6) Write notes on any TWO of the following minor characters in *Othello*, and show the various ways in which they contribute to the dramatic action of the play: Brabantio, Roderigo, Emilia, The Clown, the Duke of Venice.

(7) Discuss the idea of 'judgement' in *Othello*? Give examples of the occasions when particular characters are asked to make judgements, and what effect they have on the way the dramatic conflict develops.

(8) Write an essay on the subject of Othello's love for Desdemona. What are its main characteristics?

(9) Using particular examples, show how Shakespeare explores the theme of deception in *Othello*.

(10) Analyse the methods that Iago uses to persuade Othello to his point of view.

(11) Show some of the ways in which Shakespeare attempts to make Othello's fall in the play credible.

(12) Indicate some of the ways in which Shakespeare develops the 'atmosphere' of the tragic action in *Othello*. Offer specific examples in your answer.

(13) Write an essay on 'language' in *Othello*, showing both its particular uses, and what it contributes to the development of the play's themes.

(14) Show some of the ways in which Shakespeare employs dramatic irony in *Othello*.

(15) Write an essay on Shakespeare's use of poetic imagery in *Othello*.

(16) In *Othello* Shakespeare always takes care to keep before us more than one point of view. Do you agree?

(17) What is meant by the phrase 'dramatic structure'? Show how particular elements in the play contribute to its overall design.

(18) Write an essay on Shakespeare's use of soliloquy in *Othello*.

(19) Discuss critically Shakespeare's handling of the plot in *Othello*.
(20) From your reading of Act I of *Othello* show the ways in which Shakespeare integrates individual scenes into the main plot of the play.
(21) Why is Cyprus such an appropriate setting for the testing of Othello's love for Desdemona?
(22) In what ways might *Othello* be considered a 'revenge' play?

When answering essay questions, you should first read the question *carefully*. Once you are sure you understand it, you should then spend a little time (perhaps about five minutes) planning your answer. Because you will be expected to *explain* your response to the question, you will, therefore wish to advance your strongest arguments. The ordering of your ideas and the selection of suitable quotations will help you to do this.

When you are ready to write, introduce your discussion with a short paragraph explaining what you intend to do in your answer. Then lead into your first point. You should have time to make six or seven points in any one answer. If you build your argument in this way, taking a separate paragraph for each major point you have to make, and following through in each case with a detailed examination of your illustrations, then you will have no difficulty in convincing a reader that your argument is a valid one. This procedure has the added advantage of forcing you to think your ideas through, so that you can recognise difficulties for yourself, and overcome them. This is also a useful way of learning to *apply* your knowledge of a play like *Othello*. Remember that the secret of thorough study is to work your way through the play anticipating the questions which it raises. In this way you can solve most of the difficulties it poses before you answer questions in an examination.

Here are four answers which have been sketched out, and which are designed to help you to organise your own responses to the play.

Question 3: What do you consider to be the significance of Othello's death at the end of the play? Does it achieve anything?

From our critical discussion of the play, you will recognise that this is a question about the nature of its 'tragedy'. How do we respond to his death? Does it have some meaning, or is it simply wasteful and futile? Since the point of tragedy is to confront in some way the fact of death, it seems reasonable to expect that Othello's death does have some significance. These are the sorts of issues you might raise in this opening paragraph as a way of 'opening up' the question.

In the case of this question it is worth beginning at the end of the play, in Act 5 Scene 2. As a way of answering the question of why Othello kills himself, you would focus on what he says at the point where he commits suicide: 'And say besides that in Aleppo once, . . .' (V.2.353–7). Obviously he is aware of what he has done to Desdemona, and he is punishing himself as though he were the protector of Venice against the Turkish enemy. Thus he is judging himself as though he were the enemy.

This leads naturally to the question of 'justice' in the play—the way in which the forces of Law and Order are used to control the unacceptable excesses of human behaviour. We need now to think of some examples of how 'justice' is shown to be working in *Othello*, and we remember that these examples are of two kinds. Firstly, there is the figure of the Duke (I.3) who metes out justice, but only after he has made sure that he knows the facts of each case. His kind of justice provides the basis for a stable society, just as Othello's 'love' for Desdemona imposes 'order' on an otherwise chaotic universe.

The second kind of 'justice' is, ironically, the reverse of that which we have just observed. It is the kind that Iago persuades Othello to carry out on Desdemona. But Othello acts before he knows all the facts (unlike the Duke) although he does so because he believes Iago is 'honest'. Thus, although we know Othello is wrong about Desdemona, we understand why he is wrong, and we can sympathise to some extent with his motives. This ironical reversal of justice causes the tragedy.

It is Iago who stands for 'evil' in the play. He perverts the mind of each character he comes into contact with, and he represents a point towards which the fallen Othello gradually moves. Notice his description of Othello's marriage (I.1.86–91), and notice how Othello himself takes over Iago's cynically reductive attitude, to the point where the latter can allow his victim to speak for him (see IV.1.275–6). In doing so Othello rejects and then kills Desdemona, thinking all the time that he is perfectly justified in doing so. This is what Othello means at the opening of Act 5 Scene 2 when he speaks of 'It is the cause, it is the cause, my soul . . .'.

But we know that Othello is wrong, and we know why. The horror of what he has done only emerges once Iago's plots come out into the open. What therefore, does Othello *do* once he knows the truth? He does not *excuse* his deed, but takes full responsibility for it. He asks in his final speech that when these 'unlucky deeds' are re-told, then Lodovico should 'Speak of them as they are; nothing extenuate,/Nor set down aught in malice;' (V.2.343–4). But the final tragic irony is that in isolating the evil which he now recognises that he must kill in himself, he has, of course to kill that which is good also. The two cannot be separated. This leaves us in something of a dilemma since, while we acknowledge that his death is a final victory over the evil that Iago stands for, we regret that Othello has to die. His death, therefore is both a victory *and* a waste.

Our sense of regret and elation at this point is sharpened when we remind ourselves of Othello's former status as the 'noble emissary' of Venice, whom we have come to admire. We are never allowed to forget this side of his character (see IV.1.260–5). It is also the side of his character which Othello recalls just before he kills himself. Thus at the end what is re-established is his former nobility, although it is accomplished at great cost. We feel both the triumph and the sacrifice.

What, finally does Othello's death tell us? Because he never loses our sympathy completely, we do not dismiss his claims at the end. The justice that he enacted upon Desdemona he now turns upon himself in an act which requires great courage. Thus, he comes to some understanding (through a recognition of the evil in himself) of how 'good' and 'evil' are balanced in the world, and how Man can overcome his deficiencies. Othello's death is, therefore, a kind of lesson. He shows that Man can triumph over the evil which enslaves him, but the price of that triumph is death.

Question 10: Analyse the methods that Iago uses to persuade Othello to his point of view.

This is a question about 'plotting' in the play, and can be considered on a number of levels. For example, we may notice how Iago's plots are made to harmonise with the more general design of the play, in that it is upon these contrived situations that the tragic action turns. The characteristic feature of all Iago's plots is that they seek to undermine the attitudes and positions of others. Thus, from the beginning we need to view his plots in terms of his own stated objectives, as well as in terms of the methods he employs to attain them. -

There are many examples of Iago's persuasive methods at work in the play, but let us select three examples as a means of illustrating our argument. They are, his corruption of the mind of Brabantio (I.1), the ruining of Cassio's 'reputation' (II.3), and the 'poisoning' of the relationship between Othello and Desdemona. One feature which these three examples share, is that they all indicate the extent to which Iago takes care to provide an overall framework for the particular deceptions he intends to practise. Let us consider the case of Brabantio first.

Iago urges Roderigo to interrupt Brabantio's slumbers and to inform him in a particular way of the elopement of Othello and his daughter. Brabantio is to be persuaded that he has been the victim of a robbery, and he is invited to verify for himself the truth of Roderigo's allegations. Iago's method, then, is to sow doubt where before there was peace of mind, and to invite the complicity of his victim. The result is that Brabantio 'falls', he is persuaded into thinking the same things about Othello as Iago does, and, moreover, he is now prepared to act upon his newly acquired knowledge. The success of Iago's method can be judged by the way in which Brabantio takes over, not only the point of view of Iago, but also the kind of language he uses. This foreshadows what is to happen to Othello himself later in the play.

Obviously, Iago seeks to probe what he considers to be the weaknesses of others. This is clearly the case in the episode in Act II Scene 3 where he intends to take full advantage of Cassio's 'weakness'. Cassio is persuaded, much against his better judgement, to drink more wine than is good for him, and he gets involved in a brawl. Iago solicits the opinion of Montano in an attempt to provide a plausible context for Cassio's 'fall', and these new-found doubts about the lieutenant's competence seem to be confirmed when he enters in a drunken rage, driving Roderigo before him. Iago stage-manages this entire incident, which culminates in Cassio's being deprived of his office. As in the earlier episode the lies which Iago tells are made plausible by circumstantial evidence. But in the case of Cassio's downfall, it provides another strand in the plot which Iago is concerned to direct against Othello himself.

The persuasion of Othello, at Act III Scene 3, is the central point towards which these subsidiary actions have been steadily moving. Iago begins by gently sowing doubts in Othello's mind. For example, Cassio's hasty exit (III.3.35ff.) provides an impetus, and he leads Othello on with his calculated hesitation, making his victim believe that only his politeness prevents him from uttering an unacceptable truth. Thus, Othello himself now begins to doubt things which hitherto he had accepted uncritically. From this point onwards, each detail which he observes will be used to contribute to an overall point of view constructed skilfully for him by Iago. The key to Iago's success is the plausibility of his lies, and the assumption, accepted by all the other characters in the play, that he is 'honest'.

The point about Iago's honesty leads naturally into the more general question of his deception. He is a character who exploits the distinction between 'appearance' and 'reality', and who uses this to confuse the moral perspectives of others. When Iago sets to work, nothing is certain. He has a deliberately unsettling effect upon each of the characters with whom he comes into contact, and it is this capacity to disturb, while remaining plausible in his explanations, that makes him such a deadly force in the play.

Iago succeeds only so long as he can continue to prevent each of the characters he uses in his plots from coming together to discuss their actions. Only at the end of the play, after the damage has been done, does Emilia break this pattern of behaviour and speak out. Her public revelation brings together all the details of Iago's plots in a new focus, and it is this reconstructing of the pattern of events which has the effect of finally exposing Iago's method of persuasion as evil.

Question 15: Write an essay on Shakespeare's use of poetic imagery in *Othello*.

This is a question about a particular aspect of Shakespeare's dramatic technique. We may begin by observing that in the play imagery of this kind fulfils two significant functions: (*i*) particular images are used to provide 'atmosphere', giving us a vivid sense of the concrete details of things happening and (*ii*) images are arranged in 'patterns', and their cumulative effect is to present the two sides of the dramatic conflict.

Let us take the first category. In Act I Scene 3 the Duke tries to repair Brabantio's lost self-esteem by asking him to accept Desdemona's marriage and he uses an interesting image to do so: 'The robb'd that smiles, steals something from the thief,/He robs himself that spends a bootless grief.' (I.3.208–9). This image of the 'thief' reminds us immediately of Iago's cry: 'thieves, thieves, thieves' earlier in Act I, and it also draws our attention to the ambiguity of Othello's marriage. Has he stolen Desdemona? or is their marriage respectable? We must also see what *function* the Duke's image fulfils here. Is he counselling Brabantio to withstand his loss with fortitude, or is he saying that the old man's smiles would indicate that he had not been robbed at all? Thus the image admits of *two* possible interpretations, which support both the negative and the positive aspects of the case.

Let us now consider the image which Montano uses to describe the storm at the beginning of Act II: 'Methinks the wind does speak aloud at land . . .' (II.1.5–9). Here is a striking image of the storm. We might remember that in Cinthio's narrative the sea is calm when Othello and Desdemona sail to Cyprus, so that Shakespeare's innovation here may be for some dramatic purpose. The wind 'does speak aloud at land', and the blast has never before shaken 'our battlements' in this way. Montano is, of course, concerned to depict vividly the *immediate* effects of the storm, and to generate in us a concern for the safety of Desdemona and Othello. But this image points forward to the kind of tempest that will arise in the relationship between the two later in the play. Thus what we have here is both an attempt to evoke a sense of 'atmosphere', as well as to point to what is to come.

In addition to particular images of this kind—and there are many other examples in the play—there are also groups of images which, taken together, clarify for us the nature of the main conflict. Take, for example, those images which Iago uses to describe Othello and his marriage. They are largely derogatory, and seek to reduce the hero of the play to the level of an animal. (see I.1.87–91). Even when Brabantio views Othello as an 'outsider', it is always in the sense that he is an inferior, who has managed to charm his daughter by evil practices.

This kind of imagery matches the generally debased view of life—and, of women, in particular—taken by Iago and those whom he influences. For instance, he is cynical about Desdemona. This is, of course, the general viewpoint towards which Othello moves as the play develops, and signifies a radical shift in his opinions about his wife and about human nature generally.

Opposed to this use of 'low' imagery, for example animals, harlots, and devils, is one of a more positive kind. Othello, according to the view which emerges from this pattern of images is noble, and that nobility is expressed in vivid images depicting his bravery, fortitude, and tolerance. Similarly, we notice (through Cassio's comments particularly) the 'divine' image of Desdemona. The two patterns of images are opposed, and that opposition is crystallised in the 'Turk' versus 'Venetian' conflict.

How does this imagery contribute to the complexity of the dramatic action? Clearly 'divinity' and 'nobility' are vulnerable to attack from evil—Othello falls and Desdemona is killed. What kind of 'humanity' does the play therefore describe? This can best be answered by focusing upon a character like Emilia who is both loyal to Desdemona, and at the same time aware of the less positive view of humanity contained in Iago's images (see especially IV.3 for evidence of this). Thus these image patterns have a rather particular focus in that they illuminate a series of attitudes which inform the central conflict of the play.

We are now in a position to observe what these patterns of imagery actually lead to. They all find a focus in Othello himself, so that when he commits suicide it is the 'noble Moor' eliminating the 'animal' elements of his own character. The sharpness of this opposition is emphasised all the more by his final action which shows him as the protector of Venice re-enacting an episode from his own past life, which consolidated the realm against the 'malignant and a turban'd Turk' (V.2.354). When we remember that the phrase 'to turn Turk' meant 'to revert to uncivilised behaviour', then we begin to see how this final image fits into the overall pattern. It is this judicious use of imagery which informs the dramatic action throughout.

Question 22: In what ways might *Othello* be considered a 'revenge' play?

In a literal sense, *Othello* may be described as a 'revenge' play since the central action involves the hero performing what he assumes, albeit wrongly, to be a just retribution for a crime which he thinks has been committed. The plot is also initiated by Iago, who wants himself to be revenged for what he, rightly or wrongly, considers both a slight on his experience as a soldier, and (so he tells us later) his honour as a husband. From the beginning therefore, the play contains the notion of action and retribution, a notion that will shape its structure generally.

But *Othello* is no ordinary 'revenge' play, in which a stock revenger seeks justice for a crime that has actually been committed, and is prepared to violate normal judicial procedures in order to exact retribution. The crime for which Othello seeks justice has, we know, never actually been committed. Consequently, Desdemona's innocence makes her husband's treatment of her outrageous in any moral sense. The central irony of the play is that Othello, as the Governor of Cyprus, and hence as the guardian of law and order, perverts justice by committing an act for which there is neither a legal nor a moral sanction.

Let us now move on to consider more carefully the question of the unlawfulness of Othello's action. In the early part of the play, and indeed, up to the beginning of Act III, he is shown to be a character whose 'judgement' is strong enough to control his 'passion'. Like the Duke of Venice (as shown at the beginning of Act I Scene 3), he judges each situation rationally, and is both fair and impartial in his dealings.

In Act III Scene 3 we observe the gradual perversion of those positive values, as we see Othello's judgement overcome by his passion. Once Iago has convinced him of Desdemona's infidelity, he relinquishes all his moral principles and dedicates himself to revenge (see III.3.460ff.). This revenge will itself involve deception, and murder. But throughout, we never lose our sympathy for him, since we are allowed to see how it is that he comes to believe that Desdemona has been unfaithful to him.

Convinced that he is correct in his revaluation of Desdemona, he now wants to take revenge upon her body, since it is her physical beauty that he believes to be so dangerous. Othello believes that in revenging himself against Desdemona, he is actually performing an action for the more general benefit of mankind. Hence, he feels no contradiction in invoking the 'cause' of justice (V.2) although his reluctance to *name* his cause makes us very suspicious of its validity.

But Othello is an unusual revenger in that he does not want to kill Desdemona's 'soul'. He simply feels that that part of Desdemona which he believes to be offensive, her body, should be destroyed, although we know that her 'body' can not be separated from her 'soul' in such a simple way. This moral confusion leads ultimately to Othello's considering himself in paradoxical terms as 'an honourable murderer' (V.2.295). It is only after he has killed Desdemona that he realises that he has not been involved in an act of justice, and that his 'revenge' has been wild and unjustified.

Clearly, the burden of such an error is too great for Othello to bear, and so he turns upon himself the very justice for which he believed he was fighting, and commits suicide. His attempt to separate his own 'soul' from his black 'body' echoes his mistaken assumptions about Desdemona earlier, but his courageous action serves to preserve a balance at the end between 'sin' and 'retribution' which is essential to tragedy. Othello grows to tragic stature because he does not *avoid* the consequences of his mistaken action. This takes the action of the play beyond considerations of 'revenge', to the point where it touches the wider implications of the tragic theme which Shakespeare sought to explore. Thus, to see *Othello* as a 'revenge' play is to limit its scope. The revenge theme acts as a piece of scaffolding which helps to support the play's more complex structure.

Passages to learn by heart

I.1.44–65:   'You shall mark/. . . I am not what I am.'
I.1.88–93:   'Your heart is burst, . . . Arise I say.'
I.1.160–7:   'It is too true . . . are they married, think you?'
I.2.18–28:   'My services, . . . For the sea's worth.'
I.2.62–76:   'O, thou foul thief . . . palpable to thinking.'
I.3.76–89:   'Most potent, grave . . . In speaking for myself :'
I.3.248–54:   'That I did love the Moor, . . . fortunes consecrate :'
I.3.349–59:   'The food that to him . . . thou shalt enjoy/her;'
I.3.381–402:   'Thus do I ever . . . to the world's light.'
II.1.183–93:   'It gives me wonder . . . Succeeds in unknown fate.'
II.1.281–307:   'That Cassio loves her, . . . til us'd.'
II.3.195–207:   'Now by heaven/ . . . and guard of safety?'
II.3.326–43:   'And what's he then, . . . As I do now.'
III.3.110–20:   'By heaven, . . . Show me thy thought.'
III.3.267–77:   'Haply for I am black,/. . . For others' uses:'
III.3.460–9:   'Like to the Pontic sea, . . . I here engage my words.'
III.4.67–73:   ' 'Tis true, . . . maidens' hearts.'
IV.1.260–5:   'Is this the noble Moor, . . . light of brain?'
V.2.1–22:   'It is the cause, . . . she wakes.'
V.2.339–57:   'Soft you, a word or two:/. . . And smote him thus.'

Part 5

Suggestions for further reading

Recommended texts

Othello (edited by M.R. Ridley), Methuen, London, 1965
Othello (edited by G. Salgado), New Swan Shakespeare, Longmans, London, 1976.
Othello (edited by K. Muir), New Penguin Shakespeare, Harmondsworth, 1968.

Selected criticism

BRADLEY, A.C.: *Sheakespearean Tragedy*, Macmillan, London, 1904. One of the most influential critical works on Shakespeare to have appeared in the twentieth century.
EMPSON, WILLIAM: *The Structure of Complex Words*, Chatto & Windus, London, 1951. In a chapter entitled 'Honest in Othello', Empson argues that Iago is a 'realist', and that words like 'honest' underwent a change of meaning during the time that Shakespeare was writing his play.
HEILMAN, R.B.: *Magic in the Web: Action and Language in Othello*, Kentucky University Press, Kentucky, 1956. The most thorough investigation so far of the language of the play.
HOLLOWAY, JOHN: *The Story of The Night*, Routledge and Kegan Paul, London 1961. The chapter on *Othello* seeks to identify the hero of the play as a Renaissance prince, and provides a useful corrective to the view which sees Othello as a deficient character.
HAWKES, TERENCE: *Shakespeare and The Reason*, Routledge & Kegan Paul, London 1964. This contains a thorough investigation of the philosophical antecedents of the themes of 'appearance' and 'reality', and applies this knowledge to *Othello*, and to some of the other major tragedies.
HUNTER, G.K.: 'Othello and Colour Prejudice', *Proceedings of the British Academy*, Vol.LIII, 1967, pp.139–63. This investigates Elizabethan attitudes towards Moors, and deals with the symbolism of Othello's colour.

JONES, ELDRED: *Othello's Countrymen: The African in English Renaissance Drama*, Oxford University Press, London, 1965. A discussion of the dramatic treatment of 'black' characters in Elizabethan drama, with a useful enumeration of the prejudices of Elizabethan audiences.

KNIGHT, G. WILSON,: 'The Othello Music', *The Wheel of Fire,* Methuen, London, 1931. A helpful analysis of some of the peculiarities of Othello's language, and an attempt to see the play as a 'morality play'.

LEAVIS, F.R.: 'Diabolical Intellect and The Noble Hero', *The Common Pursuit*, Chatto and Windus, London, 1962. An attempt to place the blame for Othello's fall entirely on his own deficiencies of character, which, it is argued, he reveals from the very beginning. This essay was intended as a response to Bradley's approach, but it exchanges one set of misconceptions for another.

The author of these notes

JOHN DRAKAKIS was educated at University College Cardiff, where he read English and History. He then obtained a Dip. Ed., at St Luke's College, Exeter, and subsequently he returned to Cardiff to read for an M.A. in English Literature at University College, Cardiff. He spent three years lecturing in English at Trinity and All Saints' Colleges of Education in Leeds, and since then has held the post of lecturer in English Studies at the University of Stirling. He has been a visiting lecturer in the United States, in Singapore, and in Malaya. He has published articles and reviews on Shakespeare, and is the editor of a collection of essays on *British Radio Dramatists*. At present he is working on an edition of the plays of the cavalier dramatist Shackerley Marmion, and on a study of Shakespearean dialogue.

York Notes: list of titles

CHINUA ACHEBE
Things Fall Apart
EDWARD ALBEE
Who's Afraid of Virginia Woolf?
ANONYMOUS
Beowulf
Everyman
W. H. AUDEN
Selected Poems
JANE AUSTEN
Emma
Mansfield Park
Northanger Abbey
Persuasion
Pride and Prejudice
Sense and Sensibility
SAMUEL BECKETT
Waiting for Godot
ARNOLD BENNETT
The Card
JOHN BETJEMAN
Selected Poems
WILLIAM BLAKE
Songs of Innocence, Songs of Experience
ROBERT BOLT
A Man For All Seasons
HAROLD BRIGHOUSE
Hobson's Choice
ANNE BRONTË
The Tenant of Wildfell Hall
CHARLOTTE BRONTË
Jane Eyre
EMILY BRONTË
Wuthering Heights
ROBERT BROWNING
Men and Women
JOHN BUCHAN
The Thirty-Nine Steps
JOHN BUNYAN
The Pilgrim's Progress
BYRON
Selected Poems
GEOFFREY CHAUCER
Prologue to the Canterbury Tales
The Clerk's Tale
The Franklin's Tale
The Knight's Tale
The Merchant's Tale
The Miller's Tale
The Nun's Priest's Tale

The Pardoner's Tale
The Wife of Bath's Tale
Troilus and Criseyde
SAMUEL TAYLOR COLERIDGE
Selected Poems
SIR ARTHUR CONAN DOYLE
The Hound of the Baskervilles
WILLIAM CONGREVE
The Way of the World
JOSEPH CONRAD
Heart of Darkness
STEPHEN CRANE
The Red Badge of Courage
BRUCE DAWE
Selected Poems
DANIEL DEFOE
Moll Flanders
Robinson Crusoe
WALTER DE LA MARE
Selected Poems
SHELAGH DELANEY
A Taste of Honey
CHARLES DICKENS
A Tale of Two Cities
Bleak House
David Copperfield
Great Expectations
Hard Times
Oliver Twist
The Pickwick Papers
EMILY DICKINSON
Selected Poems
JOHN DONNE
Selected Poems
GERALD DURRELL
My Family and Other Animals
GEORGE ELIOT
Middlemarch
Silas Marner
The Mill on the Floss
T. S. ELIOT
Four Quartets
Murder in the Cathedral
Selected Poems
The Cocktail Party
The Waste Land
J. G. FARRELL
The Siege of Krishnapur
WILLIAM FAULKNER
The Sound and the Fury

HENRY FIELDING
Joseph Andrews
Tom Jones

F. SCOTT FITZGERALD
Tender is the Night
The Great Gatsby

GUSTAVE FLAUBERT
Madame Bovary

E. M. FORSTER
A Passage to India
Howards End

JOHN FOWLES
The French Lieutenant's Woman

JOHN GALSWORTHY
Strife

MRS GASKELL
North and South

WILLIAM GOLDING
Lord of the Flies
The Spire

OLIVER GOLDSMITH
She Stoops to Conquer
The Vicar of Wakefield

ROBERT GRAVES
Goodbye to All That

GRAHAM GREENE
Brighton Rock
The Heart of the Matter
The Power and the Glory

WILLIS HALL
The Long and the Short and the Tall

THOMAS HARDY
Far from the Madding Crowd
Jude the Obscure
Selected Poems
Tess of the D'Urbervilles
The Mayor of Casterbridge
The Return of the Native
The Woodlanders

L. P. HARTLEY
The Go-Between

NATHANIEL HAWTHORNE
The Scarlet Letter

SEAMUS HEANEY
Selected Poems

ERNEST HEMINGWAY
A Farewell to Arms
The Old Man and the Sea

SUSAN HILL
I'm the King of the Castle

BARRY HINES
Kes

HOMER
The Iliad
The Odyssey

GERARD MANLEY HOPKINS
Selected Poems

TED HUGHES
Selected Poems

ALDOUS HUXLEY
Brave New World

HENRIK IBSEN
A Doll's House

HENRY JAMES
The Portrait of a Lady
Washington Square

BEN JONSON
The Alchemist
Volpone

JAMES JOYCE
A Portrait of the Artist as a Young Man
Dubliners

JOHN KEATS
Selected Poems

PHILIP LARKIN
Selected Poems

D. H. LAWRENCE
Selected Short Stories
Sons and Lovers
The Rainbow
Women in Love

HARPER LEE
To Kill a Mocking-Bird

LAURIE LEE
Cider with Rosie

CHRISTOPHER MARLOWE
Doctor Faustus

HERMAN MELVILLE
Moby Dick

THOMAS MIDDLETON *and*
WILLIAM ROWLEY
The Changeling

ARTHUR MILLER
A View from the Bridge
Death of a Salesman
The Crucible

JOHN MILTON
Paradise Lost I & II
Paradise Lost IV & IX
Selected Poems

V. S. NAIPAUL
A House for Mr Biswas

ROBERT O'BRIEN
Z for Zachariah

SEAN O'CASEY
Juno and the Paycock

GEORGE ORWELL
Animal Farm
Nineteen Eighty-four

JOHN OSBORNE
Look Back in Anger
WILFRED OWEN
Selected Poems
ALAN PATON
Cry, The Beloved Country
THOMAS LOVE PEACOCK
Nightmare Abbey and *Crotchet Castle*
HAROLD PINTER
The Caretaker
SYLVIA PLATH
Selected Works
PLATO
The Republic
ALEXANDER POPE
Selected Poems
J. B. PRIESTLEY
An Inspector Calls
WILLIAM SHAKESPEARE
A Midsummer Night's Dream
Antony and Cleopatra
As You Like It
Coriolanus
Hamlet
Henry IV Part I
Henry IV Part II
Henry V
Julius Caesar
King Lear
Macbeth
Measure for Measure
Much Ado About Nothing
Othello
Richard II
Richard III
Romeo and Juliet
Sonnets
The Merchant of Venice
The Taming of the Shrew
The Tempest
The Winter's Tale
Troilus and Cressida
Twelfth Night
GEORGE BERNARD SHAW
Arms and the Man
Candida
Pygmalion
Saint Joan
The Devil's Disciple
MARY SHELLEY
Frankenstein
PERCY BYSSHE SHELLEY
Selected Poems
RICHARD BRINSLEY SHERIDAN
The Rivals

R. C. SHERRIFF
Journey's End
JOHN STEINBECK
Of Mice and Men
The Grapes of Wrath
The Pearl
LAURENCE STERNE
A Sentimental Journey
Tristram Shandy
TOM STOPPARD
Professional Foul
Rosencrantz and Guildenstern are Dead
JONATHAN SWIFT
Gulliver's Travels
JOHN MILLINGTON SYNGE
The Playboy of the Western World
TENNYSON
Selected Poems
W. M. THACKERAY
Vanity Fair
J. R. R. TOLKIEN
The Hobbit
MARK TWAIN
Huckleberry Finn
Tom Sawyer
VIRGIL
The Aeneid
ALICE WALKER
The Color Purple
KEITH WATERHOUSE
Billy Liar
EVELYN WAUGH
Decline and Fall
JOHN WEBSTER
The Duchess of Malfi
OSCAR WILDE
The Importance of Being Earnest
THORNTON WILDER
Our Town
TENNESSEE WILLIAMS
The Glass Menagerie
VIRGINIA WOOLF
Mrs Dalloway
To the Lighthouse
WILLIAM WORDSWORTH
Selected Poems
WILLIAM WYCHERLEY
The Country Wife
W. B. YEATS
Selected Poems